Michael Friedländer

Text-Book of the Jewish Religion

Michael Friedländer

Text-Book of the Jewish Religion

ISBN/EAN: 9783337033002

Printed in Europe, USA, Canada, Australia, Japan

Cover: Foto ©Lupo / pixelio.de

More available books at **www.hansebooks.com**

OF

THE JEWISH RELIGION.

BY

M. FRIEDLÄNDER.

LONDON
KEGAN PAUL, TRENCH, TRÜBNER, & CO., L™
1890.

PREFACE.

The Text-Book of the Jewish Religion which is herewith offered to the Jewish public is an outline of a larger work which the author has prepared on the same subject. It is, however, complete in itself, and contains as much as we should like our younger children to know of our Holy Religion. Due regard has been paid to the Chief Rabbi's Code, which determined the substance and the form of this volume. A complete index shows how to use it for each standard; but the author did not deem it advisable to restrict the book exclusively to the requirements of the Code. The latter may be modified; the progress of the Hebrew classes may, and we hope will, in course of time demand a higher standard. It was, therefore, preferred to give a short but complete exposition of the principles and the precepts of our Religion, in such a manner that the book may also be used as a guide for more advanced pupils.

The analysis of the Prayer-Book will be found

useful in teaching and learning the translation of the Prayers. It will facilitate the comprehension of the spirit and object of our Prayers, the general contents of which will thus be easily retained in memory even when the meaning of the single words is forgotten.

In expounding the meaning of the various observances in our religious life, it has been the aim of the author to kindle and to keep alive within the hearts of the younger generation feelings of love and respect for that Holy Faith which is the most precious treasure their elders have to offer them.

The short form of Prayer prefixed to the Text-Book may serve as a not inappropriate beginning or conclusion to each religious lesson.

In conclusion, I beg to tender my best thanks to the Rev. S. Singer, who kindly placed his valuable services at my disposal for the revision of this volume.

M. FRIEDLÄNDER.

Jews' College, *Heshvan* 5650.

CONTENTS.

	PAGE
SHORT FORM OF COMMANDMENTS, WITH EXPLANATIONS. FOR INFANTS AND FIRST STANDARD	1
TEN COMMANDMENTS, WITH EXPLANATIONS. FOR STANDARD II.	5
THE FESTIVALS. FOR STANDARD II.	10
SABBATH AND FESTIVALS. FOR STANDARDS III., IV., AND V.	13–30
Sabbath and Festivals : General Principles	13
Sabbath	15
The Festivals	17–30
יָמִים נוֹרָאִים, Solemn Days	17–22
New-Year	18
Day of Atonement	20
שָׁלשׁ רְגָלִים, The Three Festivals	22–30
Passover	23
The Seder	25
The Counting of the Omer	27
Feast of Weeks	28
Tabernacles	28
HISTORICAL FEASTS AND FASTS	30–33
חֲנוּכָּה, Feast of Dedication	31
Purim	32
The Four Fasts	32
TEXTS OF MORAL DUTIES, IN ENGLISH	34
TEXTS OF MORAL DUTIES, IN HEBREW—APPENDIX V.	94
THE THIRTEEN PRINCIPLES OF FAITH	37–52
Principles I.–IV.—God and His Attributes	37–43
First Principle : God the Creator	38
The Attributes of God	39

CONTENTS.

	PAGE
Second Principle: Unity of God	39
Third Principle: Incorporeality of God	40
His Omnipresence and Omniscience	41
Fourth Principle: Eternity of God	41
Fifth Principle: Omnipotence of God	41
His Kindness and Goodness	42
His Justice	42
His Holiness and Perfection	43
Principles VI.–IX.—Revelation and Prophecy	43–46
Sixth Principle: Prophets	44
Seventh Principle: Moses and his Prophetic Mission	44
Eighth Principle: Integrity of the Torah	45
Ninth Principle: Immutability of the Divine Law	45
Principles X.–XIII.—Providence and Justice	46–52
Tenth Principle: Omniscience of God	46
Eleventh Principle: God's Justice	47
Twelfth Principle: Messiah	48
Thirteenth Principle: The Immortality of the Soul—Future Life	50
DIVINE WORSHIP	53–59
General Principles	53
Prayers at Fixed Times	54–58
The Shema	55
The Amidah, or Eighteen Benedictions	56
Morning Service	57
Musaph, Minchah, and Neïlah	58
Evening Prayer	58
Occasional Prayers	58–59
Benedictions	58
Grace, בִּרְכַּת הַמָּזוֹן	59
OUTWARD SIGNS AS REMINDERS OF GOD'S PRESENCE	60–63
Mezuzah	60
צִיצִת	61
Tefillin	61
SIGNS OF GOD'S COVENANT	63
MORAL DUTIES	64–75
Duties towards God	64–66
Fear and Love of God	64

	PAGE
Faith in God	65
Obedience	65
Devotion	65
Longing for Reconciliation with God	65
Duties to our Fellow-Creatures	66-74
Duties to our Fellow-Men	66-73
(a) General Duties	66-69
Love of our Fellow-Men	66
Honesty and Truth	67
Charity	68
(b) Special Duties	69-73
Children towards their Parents	69
Friends towards each other	70
Husband and Wife towards each other	70
Citizens towards the State	71
Individuals towards the Community	71
Duties towards Members of another Faith	71
Towards Teachers, Scholars, the Old, the Sovereign and the Government	72
Towards the Memory of Great and Good Men	72
Kindness to Animals	73
Duties to Ourselves	74
THE DIETARY LAWS	78
TRADITION	81
THE JEWISH CALENDAR	83

APPENDICES.

I. The Jewish Calendar	85
II. The Books of the Bible and Apocrypha	88
III. Hebrew Text of the Ten Commandments	92
IV. Hebrew Text of the Thirteen Principles	93
V. Texts of Moral Duties in Hebrew	94
VI. Benedictions—Hebrew and English	96

THE STANDARDS.

		PAGE
Infants. Short Form of Ten Commandments (only the paragraphs printed in Italics)		1-4
Standard I. The same, with Explanations		1-4
„ II. Commmandments, with Explanations		5-9
Sabbath and Festivals		10-12
Historical Feasts and Fasts (only the paragraphs printed in Italics)		30-33
„ III. Sabbath and Festivals (the paragraphs printed in Italics)		13-30
Texts of Moral Duties		34-36
„ IV. The Thirteen Principles (all except the notes)		37-52
Love and Reverence of God		64-66
Sabbath and Festivals; Historical Feasts and Fasts (all except the notes)		13-33
Divine Worship (all except the notes)		53-59
צִיצָת, מְזוּזָה		60-61
Respect for Parents		69-70
Respect for Teachers, and the Aged		72
Love of our Neighbour; Honesty and Truthfulness		66-68
„ V. The Calendar and Observances of each Festival (all, including notes)		13-33
Dietary Laws		78-80
Duties to our Neighbour		66-73
Kindness to Animals		73-74
תְּפִלִּין		61-63
VI. Attributes of God		39-43
Prophecy		43-46
Future Life		50-52
תְּפִלִּין		61-63
Loyalty		71
Messiah		48-50
The Seder		25-27
Tradition		81-83

אֲדֹנָי הַעֲרֶב־נָא אֶת־ דִּבְרֵי תוֹרָתְךָ בְּפִינוּ וְנִהְיֶה יוֹדְעֵי שְׁמֶךָ וּלְמָדֵי תוֹרָתֶךָ וְיַחֵד לְבָבֵנוּ לְאַהֲבָה וּלְיִרְאָה אֶת־ שְׁמֶךָ : אָמֵן

O Lord! let the words of Thy Law be pleasant in our mouth. May we know Thy Name, and study Thy Law. Unite our hearts in the love and the reverence of Thy Name. Amen.

TEXT-BOOK

OF THE

JEWISH RELIGION.

SHORT FORM OF COMMANDMENTS,

WITH EXPLANATIONS.

(FOR INFANTS AND FIRST STANDARD.)

I. *I am the Lord thy God, who brought thee out of the land of Egypt, out of the house of bondage.*[1]

These words were spoken by the Almighty to the Israelites, the same people who had been kept as slaves in Egypt, and who, through the mercy and goodness of the Almighty, were now standing as free men round Mount Sinai. Remembering what God did for our fathers at that time, we Jews ought to love God and obey His commandments.

II. *Thou shalt have no other gods before me.*

There is only one God. In our morning and evening prayers we say, "Hear, O Israel, the Lord is our

---

[1] A house of bondage is a house in which people are forced to work like slaves.

God, the Lord is One." It is a great sin to offer up a prayer to any other being or to worship it as God. The things so worshipped are called idols, and those who sin in this way are called idol-worshippers, or idolaters, or heathen people.

III. *Thou shalt not take the name of the Lord thy God in vain.*
God is Holy, and His name is holy. We must bear this in mind whenever we utter the name of God, whether in prayer, or in reading the Bible, or in our lessons, or on other occasions. The third commandment tells us that we must not swear falsely, or even unnecessarily. If we pray without devotion, or read the Bible without attention, we sin and take the name of God in vain.

IV. *Remember the Sabbath day to keep it holy. Six days shalt thou labour and do all thy work: but the seventh day is a sabbath unto the Lord thy God: in it thou shalt not do any work.*
Sabbath is a Hebrew word and means "rest" and "day of rest." From Friday evening, when Sabbath comes in, to Saturday night we must do no manner of work. We must not be lazy or idle, but must devote our time partly to prayer, reading the Bible, and listening to religious instruction, and partly to exercise and amusement. Sabbath is to us a day of holiness and cheerfulness.

V. *Honour thy father and thy mother.*
Children ought to find it easy to obey this command-

ment. They need only think of the goodness of their parents: how much they are loved by their parents; what amount of care and trouble the parents take to make their children happy. Children who bear this in mind love their parents, try to make them happy by being good and obedient, and thus please the Almighty, who commanded us to honour our parents.

VI. *Thou shalt not murder.*
The most precious gift the Almighty has given us is life. To destroy the life of our fellow-man is a shocking thing. We must try our best to preserve and save life; we must nurse the sick, and save those whom we see in danger.

VII. *Thou shalt not commit adultery.*
This commandment tells us that husband and wife must not be false or faithless one to the other. They must love, respect, and trust each other, and do everything in their power to make each other happy.

VIII. *Thou shalt not steal.*
We must not take that which belongs to another. It is not only stealing that is prohibited, but all kinds of cheating; finding things lost by another and not returning them to the rightful owner; borrowing things and not returning them; taking things from home secretly without the permission or consent of the parents: all these and similar acts are crimes forbidden by the eighth commandment.

IX. *Thou shalt not bear false witness against thy neighbour.*

This commandment forbids us to say anything of our neighbour that is not true. Nothing but the strict truth must be spoken, whether we speak to our parents, or to our teachers, or to our schoolfellows, or to any one else. We must not flatter and we must not slander; that is, we may not say nice things to another person, nor bad things about him, if they are not true.

X. *Thou shalt not covet.*[1]

We must not wish to get that which belongs to another; we ought to be contented with that which the Almighty has given us. We must not be selfish and imagine that we must have the nicest and best things; our fellow-men are, like ourselves, children of God, and we should let them enjoy what God has given them without envying them.

[1] To covet means to wish to have.

THE TEN COMMANDMENTS,

WITH EXPLANATIONS.

(FOR STANDARD II.)

First Commandment.

I am the Lord thy God, who brought thee out of the land of Egypt, out of the house of bondage.

This commandment teaches us the following three lessons:—

1. God has shown great kindness to our nation. We Jews must therefore, more than other people, show ourselves grateful to Him, love Him as our Deliverer and Benefactor, and do willingly all that He commands us to do.

2. When we are in trouble we must trust in God, pray to Him, and hope that He will help us. Even if our fellow-men cannot help us, and give us up as lost, we need not despair, for the Almighty can help where human wisdom and power are insufficient.

3. The wicked may succeed for a time in doing wrong, whilst the good and just suffer; but this does not last for ever. There is a Master over all of us, who in due time punishes the wicked and saves the good.

Second Commandment.

Thou shalt have no other gods before me. Thou shalt not make unto thee a graven image; nor the form of any-

thing that is in heaven above, or that is in the earth beneath, or that is in the water under the earth. Thou shalt not bow down thyself unto them, nor serve them; for I the Lord thy God am a jealous God, visiting the iniquity of the fathers upon the children, upon the third and upon the fourth generation of them that hate me, and showing loving-kindness to the thousandth generation, unto them that love me and keep my commandments.

This commandment, in forbidding all kinds of idolatry, forbids the following things:—

1. The worship of sun, moon, stars, animals, or any part of Nature as if it were endowed with divine power.
2. The worship of images representing things that exist in reality or things that only exist in man's imagination.
3. The worship of angels. They are only messengers of God, and not gods.
4. The belief in evil spirits, demons, devils, and the like, and the fear of them.
5. The belief in charms, witchcraft, fortune-telling, and similar superstitions.

Third Commandment.

Thou shalt not take the name of the Lord thy God in vain; for the Lord will not hold him guiltless that taketh His name in vain.

This commandment forbids us:—

1. To utter the name of God unnecessarily in our ordinary conversation.
2. To be careless and thoughtless when reading the Bible or praying.

3. To swear otherwise than when required by the law to do so, as, *e.g.*, in courts of law by the direction of the judges or magistrates.

4. To swear when we are not fully convinced of the truth of our declaration.

5. To break any promise of ours, especially if we have made it on oath.

Fourth Commandment.

Remember the Sabbath day to keep it holy. Six days shalt thou labour, and do all thy work: but the seventh day is a sabbath unto the Lord thy God: in it thou shalt not do any work, thou, nor thy son, nor thy daughter, thy man-servant, nor thy maid-servant, nor thy cattle, nor thy stranger that is within thy gates: for in six days the Lord made heaven and earth, the sea and all that is therein, and rested the seventh day: wherefore the Lord blessed the Sabbath day and hallowed it.

The Sabbath is to be kept holy. In two ways it is therefore different from the other days: the Sabbath is a day of rest, and a holy day. We keep it as a day of rest by not doing any kind of work; we keep it as a holy day by devoting a great part of it to reading and studying the Word of God and to prayers.

The fourth commandment tells us—

1. To remember to keep the same day as Sabbath which has been appointed as Sabbath from the beginning; that is, the seventh day.

2. To abstain on that day from all kind of work.

3. To devote part of the day to Divine Service.

4. To observe the Sabbath as a day of blessing and cheerfulness.

Fifth Commandment.

Honour thy father and thy mother, that thy days may be long upon the land which the Lord thy God giveth thee.

We obey the fifth commandment—

1. By listening respectfully to the words of our parents, and minding what they tell us.
2. By doing that which pleases them, and avoiding that which displeases them.
3. By supporting them willingly and generously when they are weak or poor.
4. By honouring their name and memory after their death.
5. By being obedient to our elder brothers and sisters, to our guardians, and to our teachers, who carry out the wish of our parents.

Sixth Commandment.

Thou shalt not murder.

This commandment enjoins the duty of respecting the life of our fellow-man, and forbids us—

1. To take any man's life by violent means.
2. To do anything by which the health, peace, and well-being of our fellow-man might be undermined.
3. To neglect anything in our power to save our neighbour from direct or indirect danger of life.

Seventh Commandment.

Thou shalt not commit adultery.

. This prohibition comprehends—

1. All acts of faithlessness of a man to his wife, and of a woman to her husband.
2. The use of bad and low language.
3. Immodest conduct.
4. Associating with low and loose persons.

Eighth Commandment.

Thou shalt not steal.
This commandment forbids—
1. All kinds of theft and robbery.
2. All kinds of fraud and dishonesty.

Ninth Commandment.

Thou shalt not bear false witness against thy neighbour.
This commandment implies the prohibition of all kinds of falsehood against our fellow-men, whether it be in a court of justice or in ordinary conversation.

Tenth Commandment.

Thou shalt not covet thy neighbour's house; thou shalt not covet thy neighbour's wife, nor his man-servant, nor his maid-servant, nor his ox, nor his ass, nor any thing that is thy neighbour's.
The tenth commandment—
1. Forbids us to covet that which does not belong to us; and
2. Commands us to suppress any such desire when it rises in our heart.

THE FESTIVALS.

מוֹעֲדֵי יְיָ

(FOR STANDARD II.)

There are five Festivals or Holy days in the course of the year. They are divided into יָמִים נוֹרָאִים "Solemn days," and שָׁלֹשׁ רְגָלִים Three Festivals of Rejoicing.

I. יָמִים נוֹרָאִים SOLEMN DAYS.

The "Solemn days" include two Holy days, which form the beginning and the end of *Ten penitential days*," עֲשֶׂרֶת יְמֵי תְשׁוּבָה; on these days we are to reflect on our past conduct, regret our shortcomings, and resolve to improve.

1. רֹאשׁ הַשָּׁנָה *New Year*, is kept on the first and on the second days of the Hebrew month Tishri. The 1st of Tishri is the beginning of the year in the Jewish Calendar. The *Shofar* (made of the horn of a ram) is blown on New Year's Day, to remind us of our duty to begin a new life, to abandon all sinful thoughts, to mend where we have acted wrongly, and to try to be good in every respect.

2. יוֹם כִּפּוּר *Day of Atonement*, is kept on the 10th of Tishri. It is the most important and most solemn day of the year; it is a day of fasting, devotion, and

repentance. We confess our sins before the Almighty, and pray to Him for forgiveness. We are told in the Bible, "For on this day He will forgive you, to purify you; you shall be purified before the Lord of all your sins" (Lev. xvi. 30).

II. שָׁלשׁ רְגָלִים THREE FESTIVALS.

The literal meaning of the term שָׁלשׁ רְגָלִים is "three times." The two words form the beginning of the commandment concerning the three Festivals (Exod. xxiii. 14). They signify also "three pilgrimages," and in former days, when the Temple in Jerusalem was still in existence, a pilgrimage to Jerusalem was connected with the celebration of these Festivals.

1. פֶּסַח *Passover*.

Passover is kept for eight days, beginning the 15th of Nisan, in commemoration of the wonderful deliverance of the Israelites from Egyptian slavery. It is called *Passover* for this reason: the last of the ten plagues which God sent as a punishment over Egypt was the slaying of the first-born. There was not a house of the Egyptians in which some one had not died; but the houses of the Israelites were *passed over* by the plague, and no death occurred in them.

During Passover we must not eat חָמֵץ "leavened bread;" instead of leavened we eat מַצָּה "unleavened bread," in commemoration of the unleavened bread which the Israelites ate when leaving Egypt; they had to leave hurriedly, and had no time for preparing leavened bread. Therefore Passover is also called חַג הַמַּצּוֹת "Festival of Unleavened Bread."

2. שָׁבוּעוֹת *Feast of Weeks.*

The Feast of Weeks is kept on the sixth and the seventh days of Sivan. It is called Festival of Weeks because seven weeks are counted between the second day of Passover and this festival. On the second day of Passover an Omer (that is, a certain measure) of new barley was offered in the Temple as thanksgiving for the harvest which commenced in Palestine about the time of Passover. The counting is called "the counting of the Omer" סְפִירַת הָעוֹמֶר

שָׁבוּעוֹת is the anniversary of the Giving of the Law on Mount Sinai.

3. סֻכּוֹת *Feast of Tabernacles.*

This festival is kept from the 15th to the 23rd of Tishri. On the first seven days we take our meals in a booth called Sukkah or Tabernacle, in commemoration of the wanderings of the children of Israel in the wilderness, where they could not build houses, but had to live in tents, and enjoyed the special protection of the Almighty.

Tabernacles is also the Feast of Ingathering, and while singing praises to the Giver of all good things, we hold in our hands four kinds of plants: לוּלָב branch of palm-tree; אֶתְרוֹג citron; הֲדַסִּים myrtles; and עֲרָבוֹת willows of the brook.

The eighth day is called שְׁמִינִי עֲצֶרֶת "Eighth day Festival;" and the ninth day is celebrated as שִׂמְחַת תּוֹרָה "Rejoicing of the Law." We read the whole Pentateuch in the course of a year, one portion or *Sidra* being read every Sabbath. On the "Rejoicing of the Law" the last portion of the Pentateuch is read.

SABBATH AND FESTIVALS.

שַׁבָּת וּמוֹעֲדִים

(FOR STANDARDS III., IV., AND V.)

There shall be seasons of the Lord, which ye shall proclaim to be holy convocations (Lev. xxiii. 2).

Sabbath and Festivals are called מוֹעֲדֵי יְיָ "the seasons of the Lord," and מִקְרָאֵי קֹדֶשׁ "holy convocations." They are days appointed by the Lord and to be devoted to the Lord. On these days we assemble in places of worship for the purpose of sanctifying our lives.

We celebrate Sabbath and Festivals—

1. By a general cessation from our ordinary work.

NOTE.—In the Pentateuch the term מְלָאכָה "work" frequently occurs in connection with Commandments concerning Sabbath and Festivals; but no explanation is given of the meaning of the word "work." A few instances, however, are mentioned of the kind of work that is prohibited: baking, cooking, gathering manna, gathering sticks, kindling fire, carrying burdens, doing business. The Oral Law (Mishnah Sabbath, vii.) enumerates the various kinds of work or occupation that must not be engaged in on the day of rest. There is also a certain kind of work that is not directly prohibited, and yet ought not to be done on Sabbath or Festival, namely, such work as is found by our conscience to be inappropriate for the holy day. It is, e.g., no work to carry a chair from one room to another; but removing the whole furniture from one room to another would amount to a desecration of the Sabbath. All that is prohibited on Sabbath is prohibited on the Festivals, with the exception of the preparation of the food required for the day. When a Holy day happens to be on Friday the food for Sabbath may be prepared on the Holy day, provided something has been prepared for Sabbath before the Holy day commenced, and this preparation is called עֵרוּב תַּבְשִׁילִין, that is, a combination of the food prepared for Sabbath before the Holy day and that prepared on the Holy day. The עֵרוּב תַּבְשִׁילִין is accompanied by a Blessing and a statement of its object.

2. By a solemn greeting of these days at their coming, and a farewell blessing at their departure. The former is called קִדּוּשׁ, "sanctification," the latter הַבְדָּלָה, "distinction," because in it we bless God for the distinction He has made between days which are holy and days which are not holy.

NOTE.—The *Kiddush* precedes the evening meal, and consists of a blessing over wine or bread, and a blessing expressing our gratitude to the Almighty for the sanctification of the day. On Festivals, with the exception of the last days of Passover, a third blessing is added, called שֶׁהֶחֱיָנוּ, in which we thank God for having given us life and enabled us to celebrate the festival.

The *Habdalah* consists of a blessing over wine, and a blessing in which we express our thanks to the Almighty for having made a distinction between the sacred day and the ordinary day on which the restrictions with regard to work are removed. On Sabbath evening two other blessings are added; the one over spices, the other over light. The former is omitted when Sabbath is followed by a Festival.

3. By outward distinction in our dress and our meals. Our meals on these occasions are preceded and followed by appropriate psalms and hymns.

NOTE.—Extra lights are prepared for Sabbath before Sabbath comes in, and on kindling them an appropriate blessing is said. The same applies to Festivals. This act is the peculiar duty and privilege—מִצְוָה—of the housewife or her representative, as is also the following:—

Special loaves of bread are prepared for Sabbath and Festivals, and in commemoration of the commandment of Numb. xv. 17-21 it is the custom to separate a small piece of the dough or bread as חַלָּה, whilst saying an appropriate בְּרָכָה, and subsequently to burn the piece so separated.

4. By devoting on these days more time than on ordinary days to divine worship, reading from the Pentateuch and the Prophets, and attending religious instruction given by the Preacher and the Teacher.

NOTE.—The reading from the Law and the Prophets takes place between the Morning and the Additional Services (between שַׁחֲרִית and מוּסָף). On Sabbath a portion of the Law is read called *Sidra*, or weekly portion, which is divided into seven *parshiyoth* or "*sections.*" The whole of the Law is read in the course of a year (p. 12). On Holy days such portions from the Law are read as have reference to the institutions or characteristics of the day.

The portion from the Prophets is called הַפְטָרָה, "conclusion," and it has always either directly or indirectly some bearing on the portion read from the Law.

5. By thinking about our conduct; seeking to improve, and to keep our heart free from levity, vanity, arrogance, and similar vices; and directing our mind to pure and cheerful thoughts.

SABBATH שַׁבָּת

The keeping of Sabbath is enjoined in the fourth of the Ten Commandments (p. 7).

The Sabbath, commanded in connection with the manna, again enjoined in the Ten Commandments, and repeatedly emphasised in the Bible, is to be kept as an everlasting covenant, בְּרִית עוֹלָם, *and as a* sign, אוֹת, of our faith in God, the Creator of the Universe.

"And the children of Israel shall keep the Sabbath, to observe the Sabbath throughout their generations, for a perpetual covenant. It is a sign between Me and the children of Israel for ever: for in six days the Lord made heaven and earth, and on the seventh day He rested, and was refreshed" (Exod. xxxi. 16, 17).

"And God blessed the seventh day, and sanctified it: because in it He had rested from all His work which God created and made" (Gen. ii. 3).

The blessing and the holiness of the Sabbath were shown to the Israelites on the occasion of the manna. When this "food from heaven" was provided for them during their journeying from Egypt to Palestine, a certain measure, an *omer*, was collected every day for each person; but on Fridays there was sufficient manna for a double portion, while on Sabbath no manna was found. The Israelites were thus taught to provide during the weekdays for the wants of Sabbath, and they were distinctly told "To-morrow (the seventh day) is the rest of the holy Sabbath unto the Lord; bake that which you will bake to-day, and seethe that which you will seethe; and that which remaineth over lay up for you to be kept until the morning" (Exod. xvi. 23). "Ye shall kindle no fire throughout your habitations on the Sabbath day" (*Ibid.* xxxv. 3).

Jeremiah exhorts his brethren as follows: "Thus saith the Lord, Take heed to yourselves and bear no burden on the Sabbath day, nor bring it in by the gates of Jerusalem; neither carry forth a burden out of your houses on the Sabbath day, neither do you any work, but hallow ye the Sabbath day" (Jer. xvii. 21, *sqq.*).

Isaiah, speaking of the sanctity of the Sabbath, says: "If thou turn away thy foot because of the Sabbath from doing thy work on My holy day, and call the Sabbath a delight, the holy of the Lord honourable; and shalt honour it, not doing thine own ways, nor finding thine own business, nor speaking thine own word: then shalt thou delight thyself in the Lord" (Isa. lviii. 13).

"And it shall come to pass that every new moon and every Sabbath shall all flesh come to worship before Me, saith the Lord" (*Ibid.* lxvi. 23). To those that do not keep Sabbath and Festival in the proper way the prophet says: "Your new moons and your festivals my soul hateth; they have become a burden unto me" (Isa. i. 14).

The Festivals (מוֹעֲדִים or יָמִים טוֹבִים).

"*These are the set feasts of the Lord, even holy convocations, which ye shall proclaim in their appointed seasons*" (Lev. xxiii. 4).

There are five festivals, which are divided into two groups, יָמִים נוֹרָאִים "*solemn days,*" *and* שָׁלשׁ רְגָלִים "*Three festivals of rejoicing.*"

1. יָמִים נוֹרָאִים "*Solemn days.*"

Two of the five festivals are called יָמִים נוֹרָאִים, *viz.*, ראשׁ הַשָּׁנָה "*New-year;*" *and* יוֹם כִּפּוּר "*Day of Atonement.*"

ראֹשׁ הַשָּׁנָה "*New-year.*"

The first and the second days of Tishri are kept as New-year.

NOTE 1.—Although Nisan, the month of the departure of the Israelites from Egypt, is the first month, and Passover the first of the festivals of the year, Tishri, the seventh month, was in many respects the beginning of the year. In the month of Tishri the Jubilee year commenced, the slaves were liberated, and the landed property returned to the rightful owner.

NOTE 2.—In the Law only the first and the seventh day of Passover, the first day of the Feast of Weeks, the first of Tishri, and the first and the eighth days of Tabernacles are commanded to be strictly kept as "holy convocations." Originally the first of the month was determined by direct observation. The day on which the new moon was first seen was proclaimed by the Sanhedrin to be New-moon day, ראֹשׁ חֹדֶשׁ. Signals or messengers informed the congregations of the decision of the Sanhedrin. Those congregations that were too far to be reached by signals or messengers before the Holy day that happened to be in the month, kept two days instead of one, in order to be sure that the right day as determined by the decision of the Sanhedrin was celebrated as Holy day. The exact period when the second Holy day was introduced, is unknown. Wherever it is mentioned in the Talmud it occurs already as an old institution. An anxious and pious desire to observe the command of God was the source of the institution. Even when calculation took the place of observation, the congregations outside Palestine which had previously kept two days continued to do so, in order to be quite sure that even if the old system were still in force the right day would not be missed. The institution, founded on piety, willingly accepted by all the congregations, and preserved intact throughout periods of trouble and misery, cannot be abolished except by the will of the whole nation, and with the sanction of a Sanhedrin recognised by all Jews as the chief authority in religious matters.

In accordance with the lesson implied in the command: "The first of the first-fruits of thy land thou shalt bring unto the house of the Lord thy God" (Exod. xxxiv. 26), we bring the first ten days of the year an offering to the Lord; they are days of increased devotion, earnest self-examination, and new efforts to lead a good, virtuous, and godly life. They are called עֲשֶׂרֶת יְמֵי תְשׁוּבָה "ten days of return" to God, or "ten penitential days." We greet and congratulate each other on New-year, using the phrase לְשָׁנָה טוֹבָה תִּכָּתֵב "May you be inscribed for a happy year." It is a figurative expression, borrowed from the writing and signing of decrees by earthly judges.

NOTE.—Instead of תִּכָּתֵב the forms תִּכָּתְבִי, תִּכָּתְבוּ, תִּכָּתַבְנָה are used, according as a female person, several male persons, or several female persons are addressed.

This festival, being the beginning of the new year and the first of the ten penitential days, we are expected to turn over a new leaf, to abandon all sinful doing, to mend where we have acted wrongly in the past, and to resolve to be better henceforth in every respect.

The festival is called in the Torah יוֹם תְּרוּעָה *"Day of blowing the shofar," and* זִכְרוֹן תְּרוּעָה *"Memorial of the blowing of the shofar;" and in our prayers the name* יוֹם הַזִּכָּרוֹן *"Day of Remembering," and also* יוֹם הַדִּין *"Day of Judgment."*

NOTE.—We express our hopes and wishes for the coming year. Their fulfilment depends on the judgment and decree of God.

During the Morning Service the shofar is blown. The sound of the shofar is like a signal, the object of which is to awaken us to greater watchfulness and activity in the purification and sanctification of our heart.

The sound of the shofar has also to remind us of an important event which was preceded and followed by the sound of the shofar: the Revelation on Mount Sinai. As on that occasion the Israelites willingly exclaimed נַעֲשֶׂה וְנִשְׁמָע "We will do and we will hear," so we likewise are expected to repeat joyfully, "We will do and we will hear," and to proclaim God as our King, and ourselves as His faithful servants.

NOTE 1.—Our faith in God and our willingness to obey His Word are expressed in three important sections of the Musaf-prayer: שׁוֹפָרוֹת, זִכְרוֹנוֹת, מַלְכִיּוֹת, meditations on God's Kingdom, Providence, and Revelation.

NOTE 2.—The preparation for these solemn days begins with the 1st of Ellul. Extra prayers, called סְלִיחוֹת "prayers for forgiveness," are added to the ordinary service; in the Spanish Ritual during the whole of Ellul, in the German Ritual during the week preceding New-year. They are continued during the ten penitential days. The shofar is blown in the German synagogues daily during the month Ellul, after the service, in the Spanish synagogues between New-year and the Day of Atonement.

NOTE 3.—In some congregations there is a custom to walk in the afternoon of New-year along the banks of a river or the shore of the sea, in order to reflect on the purifying effect which water has on the body, and to be reminded of the necessity of seeking the means of purifying our soul—repentance and God's mercy. An appropriate passage from Micah (vii. 18–20) is recited, and the custom has received its name, תַּשְׁלִיךְ, from the word וְתַשְׁלִיךְ and thou wilt cast, which occurs in the passage.

יוֹם כִּפּוּר *Day of Atonement.*

The tenth day of the seventh month, Tishri, is the most important of all the Holy days; it is the Day of Atonement, on which " God will forgive you, declaring you purified; from all your sins before the Lord shall you purify yourselves" (Lev. xvi. 30). It is a day of fasting, praying, and repenting. We confess our sins before the Almighty, and pray to Him for forgiveness.

It is the greatest boon which we seek to obtain on this day, reconciliation with our Father in heaven; but we can only fully obtain it after having honestly sought reconciliation with our fellow-men and with ourselves.

The fasting begins on the 9th of Tishri about sunset, and lasts till the beginning of night on the following day. Thus it is said in the Pentateuch: "And this shall be a statute for ever unto you: that in the seventh month, on the tenth day of the month, ye shall afflict yourselves" (Lev. xvi. 29). "And it shall be unto you a Sabbath of rest, and ye shall afflict yourselves in the ninth day of the month, at even; from even unto even shall ye celebrate your Sabbath" (*Ibid.* xxiii. 32).

There are five services on the Day of Atonement: —1. Evening Service, מַעֲרִיב; 2. Morning Service, שַׁחֲרִית; 3. Additional Service, מוּסָף; 4. Afternoon Service, מִנְחָה; 5. Concluding Service, נְעִילָה. An essential element in all these services is the Confession, וִדּוּי. We must not merely confess our sins before the Almighty, but also regret that we have sinned, and resolve to abstain from sinning in future.

NOTE 1.—The confession of sins as contained in the Prayerbook is made by the whole community collectively; and those who have not themselves committed the sins regret that they were unable to prevent them from being committed by others.

The form of the confession is therefore in the plural, אָשַׁמְנוּ "We have been guilty."

NOTE 2.—In the Afternoon Service the Book of Jonah is read in illustration of the effect of sincere repentance.

NOTE 3.—The Sabbath before the Day of Atonement is called שַׁבָּת שׁוּבָה because the Haphtarah, taken from Hosea (xiv. 1), begins שׁוּבָה "return."

שָׁלשׁ רְגָלִים *The three Festivals of Rejoicing.*

The literal meaning of שָׁלשׁ רְגָלִים is "three times." The two words form in the Pentateuch the beginning of the commandment concerning the three festivals. They signify also "three pilgrimages," and refer to the pilgrimages to Jerusalem which were connected with these festivals before the destruction of the Temple.

These three festivals are: פֶּסַח *Passover;* שָׁבוּעוֹת *Feast of Weeks;* סֻכּוֹת *Feast of Tabernacles.*

The three festivals have also this in common, that—

1. They commemorate important events in our national history:—

Passover: the deliverance of the Israelites from the Egyptian bondage.

Feast of Weeks: the Revelation on Mount Sinai.

Feast of Tabernacles: the travels of the Israelites through the Arabian desert and the Divine protection they enjoyed.

2. They are connected with the agriculture of Palestine:—

Passover is the feast of the early harvest.

Feast of Weeks is the feast of the second harvest.

Feast of Tabernacles is the feast of the ingathering of the fruit.

3. Their celebration is also an expression of our belief in the three fundamental principles of our faith, viz. :—

Passover : the existence of the Supreme Ruler, God.
Feast of Weeks : Revelation.
Feast of Tabernacles : Providence.

פֶּסַח *Passover.*

Passover is kept eight days, from the 16th of Nisan to the 22nd. It reminds us of the wonderful deliverance of the Israelites from Egyptian slavery. When God sent the last of the ten plagues, the slaying of the first-born, as a punishment over Egypt, there was no Egyptian house where there was not a dead person, but the houses of the Israelites were passed over and no death occurred in them. It is also called זְמַן חֵרוּתֵנוּ *" The season of our liberation." When the Israelites left Egypt they went away in such haste that they had no time to prepare leavened bread; they could only take unleavened bread with them. In commemoration of this we are commanded to eat* מַצָּה, *" unleavened bread," during the festival; we are not allowed to eat any* חָמֵץ, *" leavened bread." The festival is therefore called* חַג הַמַּצוֹת *" Feast of unleavened bread."*

NOTE 1.—The various names of the festival apply to all the eight days; but only the first two and the last two days are "holy convocations:" the four middle days are called חוֹל הַמּוֹעֵד "the ordinary days of the festive season." The same is the case with the Feast of Tabernacles. The five middle days are חוֹל הַמּוֹעֵד

NOTE 2.—On שַׁבַּת חוֹל הַמּוֹעֵד of Passover, or on one of the last two days, the Song of Solomon is read in addition to the readings from the Pentateuch and the Prophets, because the Song of Solomon is interpreted as representing figuratively the history of the Israelites, including their departure from Egypt.

In obedience to the commandment, "And there shall no leavened bread be seen with thee, neither shall there be leaven seen with thee, in all thy borders" (Exod. xiii. 7), all leavened bread and everything containing any leaven is removed from the house.

NOTE 1.—On the evening between the 13th and the 14th of Nisan, בְּדִיקַת חָמֵץ "searching for the leavened bread" takes place. The house is searched, and all חָמֵץ found is collected and kept in one place till the following day. On the 14th of Nisan, עֶרֶב פֶּסַח only one meal of חָמֵץ is taken, and that in the morning; whatever חָמֵץ is then left is removed or destroyed, and this act is called בִּיעוּר חָמֵץ, "The removal of leavened bread."

NOTE 2.—The 14th of Nisan is kept by some as תַּעֲנִית בְּכוֹרִים "The fast of the first-born," first-born males fasting till mid-day or till the evening. The fast has its origin in the piety and humility of our forefathers, who doubted whether they would be worthy of God's miraculous interference in their behalf, if the country were visited by a plague like "the slaying of the first-born" in Egypt.

In commemoration of the deliverance from Egypt the Israelites were commanded to sacrifice a lamb in the afternoon of the 14th of Nisan, and to eat the flesh thereof, roasted with fire, in the evening, together with unleavened bread and bitter herbs. Since the destruction of the Temple all sacrifices have ceased; we have therefore no Paschal lamb, but we eat, before the evening meal commences, unleavened bread (מַצָּה) and bitter herbs (מָרוֹר). The latter reminds us of the bitter slavery of our forefathers in Egypt, and the מַצָּה of their wonderful deliverance.

The meal is preceded and followed by prayers, readings from the Bible and its ancient commentaries (Midrash) on the departure of the Israelites from Egypt, and singing of psalms and hymns. The book which contains this Home-Service is called הַגָּדָה "relating," *scil.* the history of the departure of the Israelites from Egypt; the whole service is called סֵדֶר, "*Order*," because it is customary to follow a fixed order in the proceedings of the evening, and the two first evenings of Passover are therefore called "Seder-evenings." It is a special duty of Jewish parents to utilise this evening service for the instruction of the young, and to inculcate into their hearts the belief in God, the Supreme Ruler of the universe.

NOTE 1.—The name הַגָּדָה is taken from the words of the commandment, "Thou shalt tell—וְהִגַּדְתָּ—thy son on that day, saying, [I do these things] because of that which the Lord did for me when I came forth out of Egypt" (Exod. xiii. 8).

NOTE 2.—The head of the family, or his substitute, who reads the service, has before him on the table—

1. Three unleavened cakes (מַצּוֹת), two representing the ordinary two loaves of bread of Sabbaths and Festivals; and one representing the "bread of affliction" (לֶחֶם עֹנִי) peculiar to the Seder-evening; this one is therefore broken into halves.

2. Vegetables (כַּרְפַּס) and salt-water, in which the vegetables are dipped.

3. Bitter herbs (מָרוֹר) and a sauce (חֲרוֹסֶת) in which the bitter herbs are dipped; the former (מָרוֹר) being a symbol of the bitter bondage of the Israelites in Egypt, the חֲרֹסֶת a symbol of the clay and mortar of which the Israelites had to make bricks.

4. Wine, of which four cups are taken in the course of the evening, as a sign of freedom and rejoicing. One cup is taken after Kiddush, one after the first part of the Hagadah, one after Grace, and one after the second part of the Hagadah. They are to

remind us of the fulness of Israel's redemption from Egypt, in reference to which four different expressions are employed in the Law וְלָקַחְתִּי, וְגָאַלְתִּי, וְהִצַּלְתִּי, וְהוֹצֵאתִי, "I will bring forth," "I will deliver," "I will redeem," and "I will take" (Exod. vi. 6-7), these various terms referring to liberation from bondage, deliverance from service, redemption from all dependence on Egypt, and appointment as "the people of the Lord." An extra cup is poured in and kept ready for any guest that might come. It is called "cup of Elijah."

5. A roasted bone and a roasted egg, as a symbol of the Paschal lamb and the festive sacrifice (פֶּסַח and חֲגִיגָה).

NOTE 3.—The order of the Service may be summarised by the following Hebrew words :—

1. קַדֵּשׁ Say Kiddush (p. xiii. b).

2. רְחַץ Washing. The reader washes his hands.

3. כַּרְפַּס A small quantity of the vegetables dipped in salt water is taken, as was anciently the general custom to do before meals.

4. יַחַץ Dividing. One of the three מַצּוֹת is divided into two; one half is put aside (p. 23, note 2).

5. מַגִּיד "Relating." The head of the family, in the paragraph beginning הָא לַחְמָא invites his guests to join the table; questions beginning מַה־נִּשְׁתַּנָּה "Why is different," are then put by one of the company, generally the youngest, with regard to the characteristics distinguishing the evening's proceedings, and the answer is supplied by the head of the family, who describes the miraculous way in which God delivered the Israelites from Egyptian bondage, and explains the object of פֶּסַח, Passover-lamb; מַצָּה unleavened bread; and מָרוֹר bitter herbs.

6. רָחְצָה Washing the hands by the whole of the company.

7. מוֹצִיא מַצָּה Two blessings are said: the ordinary blessing, הַמּוֹצִיא said before eating bread, and a second one, which refers to the commandment of eating מַצָּה. Every one then partakes of the מַצָּה.

8. כּוֹרֵךְ מָרוֹר Bitter herbs are then partaken of in two ways: first by themselves, and then together with מַצָּה.

9. שֻׁלְחָן עוֹרֵךְ Tables laid. The ordinary meal is taken.

10. צָפוּן The half מַצָּה which has been laid aside, is now distributed, so that the meal begins and ends with מַצָּה. It is called אֲפִיקוֹמָן "dessert."

11. בָּרֵךְ Say Grace.

12. הַלֵּל Hallel, of which the first two paragraphs are recited before the meal, is now completed, together with other psalms and hymns.

13. נִרְצָה Conclusion. Prayer for the restoration of the Temple and the return of the Israelites to Zion.

NOTE 4.—The songs beginning אֶחָד מִי יוֹדֵעַ and חַד גַּדְיָא have been added, to illustrate in a popular form the doctrine of the Unity of God and the lesson of His Justice.

סְפִירַת הָעוֹמֶר *The Counting of the Omer.*

Passover, being also the feast of an early harvest, an offering of an OMER *of the new barley was brought on the second day of Passover. From that day forty-nine days, or seven weeks, were counted, and on the fiftieth day, "the day of first-fruit offering" was celebrated. At present sacrifices are not offered; but the counting called* סְפִירַת הָעוֹמֶר, *"the counting of the Omer," is still observed. It begins on the second evening of Passover.*

The days between Passover and the Feast of Weeks, especially the month of Iyar, were days of sore trouble to the Jews in the time of the Roman wars during the reign of the Emperor Hadrian, and also at the period of the Crusades. We therefore abstain during the month of Iyar from wedding festivities, and the like. The 18th of Iyar, the 33rd of *Omer* (לַג בָּעֹמֶר) is excepted, because on that day the plague disappeared that had raged among the followers of Rabbi Akiba, a supporter of Barcochba, who was the leader of the Jews against the Romans.

שָׁבוּעוֹת Feast of Weeks.

The Feast of Weeks is kept on the 6th and the 7th days of Sivan. It derives its name from the counting of the seven preceding weeks. It is called יוֹם הַבִּכּוּרִים and חַג הַקָּצִיר "Day of first-fruit offering" and "Harvest-feast;" it is a day of thanksgiving for the blessings of the harvest. On שָׁבוּעוֹת we celebrate also the anniversary of the Revelation on Mount Sinai, and the festival is therefore called זְמַן מַתַּן תּוֹרָתֵנוּ, "The season of the giving of our Law."

On the first day of the festival the account of the Revelation on Mount Sinai (Exod. xix. and xx.) is read during the Morning Service. On the second day, in addition to the lessons from the Pentateuch and the Prophets, the Book of Ruth is read, and for the following reasons: first, it contains an account of the harvest and the way in which the poor were formerly allowed to glean in the fields at harvest-time; secondly, because it relates how Ruth abandoned idolatry and embraced the true faith, saying, "Thy people shall be my people, and thy God my God" (Ruth i. 16).

NOTE.—The three days preceding the festival are called שְׁלֹשֶׁת יְמֵי הַגְבָּלָה "the three days of bordering" (see Exod. xix. 12).

סֻכּוֹת Tabernacles.

The name סֻכּוֹת is used both in a wider and in a narrower sense: in the wider sense it includes the eighth and the ninth days of the festival, and in the narrower sense it applies only to the first seven days. The festival begins on the 15th of Tishri. It is called סֻכּוֹת Tabernacles, because of the commandment: "Ye shall dwell in booths seven days; all that are Israelites born shall dwell in booths" (Lev. xxiii. 42). The object of this commandment is stated thus: "That your generations may know that I made the children of Israel to dwell in booths when I brought them out of the land of Egypt" (Ibid. 43).

The booths are to remind us of the travels of the Israelites through the Arabian desert, and the Divine protection which the Israelites enjoyed.

In fulfilment of this command we erect booths or tabernacles, and if we cannot make them in every respect our dwelling, we should at least take our meals in them. It is chiefly the covering (סְכָךְ) that determines the temporary character of the Succah; it consists generally of leaves, flowers, and branches of trees.

The festival is also the feast of ingathering, חַג הָאָסִיף, and we "rejoice before the Lord" with feelings of gratitude for the blessings which He has sent us. "And ye shall take unto you on the first day the fruit of the tree hadar, branches of palm-trees, and boughs of a thick-leaved tree, and willows of the brook: and ye shall rejoice before the Lord your God seven days" (Lev. xxiii. 40).

In accordance with this commandment we take the four kinds, אַרְבָּעָה מִינִים viz., citron, אֶתְרוֹג; palm-branch, לוּלָב; myrtle, הֲדַסִּים; and willows of the brook, עֲרָבוֹת; say appropriate blessings before taking them, and keep them in our hands during the recital of Hallel.

NOTE 1.—These four species of plants represent the variety of the gifts bestowed upon us by the Almighty: one (the citron) having both a pleasant fragrance and a beautiful form; another (the palm-branch), beauty of form; the third (the myrtle), an agreeable fragrance; and the fourth (the willows of the brook), being remarkable neither for its appearance nor its odour. We are thankful to God for what He gives us, although our desires and wishes are not fully satisfied.

NOTE 2.—In ancient times the worshippers used to walk in procession round the altar with these "four kinds" in their hands. A similar custom is observed now at the end of the Musaf-Amidah. We walk round the platform (בִּימָה) in the middle of the synagogue, with lulab and esrog in our hands, while reciting certain prayers called הוֹשַׁעֲנוֹת, because the word הוֹשַׁעֲנָא "help," occurs frequently in them.

NOTE 3.—The seventh day of the festival is called הוֹשַׁעֲנָא רַבָּא because the procession round the platform in the middle of the synagogue is repeated seven times, and additional prayers beginning הוֹשַׁעֲנָא are offered. It is an old custom to take a few extra branches of the willow-tree on this day and keep them in our hand during these prayers. These branches, when shaken or struck, lose their leaves one after the other; so do the trees from which the branches have been cut, and so also all other trees. But the rain and heat sent by God in due time gives them fresh life, and they produce new leaves. A similar experience is ours. The struggle for life reduces our strength and weakens our health; cares and troubles discourage us. But faith in God and trust in His Providence renew our strength, our health improves, our cares and troubles are diminished, and we feel ourselves restored to fresh life.

The last two days of the festival are called שְׁמִינִי עֲצֶרֶת *" the Eighth-day Festival," and* שִׂמְחַת תּוֹרָה *" Rejoicing of the Law"* (see p. 12). *These two days, together with the preceding seven days, form "the season of our rejoicing,"* זְמַן שִׂמְחָתֵנוּ.

NOTE.—On שְׁמִינִי עֲצֶרֶת or on שַׁבַּת חוֹל הַמּוֹעֵד the Book of Koheleth is read, to remind us of the transient character of our life, and to teach us that the only way to true happiness is the fear of God and the obedience to His commandments.

Historical Feasts and Fasts.

Besides the festivals commanded in the Torah, we

celebrate also in the course of the year anniversaries of days of joy and days of sorrow. Of the former kind are חֲנוּכָּה and פּוּרִים; of the latter the 9th of Ab and four other fasts.

חֲנוּכָּה Feast of Dedication.

On the 25th of Kislev we begin to celebrate eight days of חֲנוּכָּה or Dedication, in commemoration of the victories of the Maccabees over Antiochus Epiphanes, king of Syria. This king had attempted to force the Jews to idolatry and to make them abandon the worship of the true God. The Jews, led by the Maccabees, resisted; and armed with faith in God they gained the victory over the large armies of the enemy. The Temple, which had been defiled by the heathen soldiers, was again purified and the service of God re-established. For lighting the continual lamp (נֵר תָּמִיד) pure oil was wanted, that had not been touched by the heathen. Only a small cruse of pure oil was found, which was believed to be sufficient for one night; but it sufficed for eight days, by which time a fresh supply could be procured.

The Feast of Dedication is celebrated—

(1.) By lighting חֲנוּכָּה lights, one on the first evening, and adding one light each successive evening, so that on the eighth evening eight lights are kindled.

(2.) By giving expression to our feeling of gratitude in psalms (הַלֵּל) and prayers of thanks (עַל הַנִּסִּים).

NOTE.—The חֲנוּכָּה lights remind us, in the first place, of the reopening of the Temple and the resumption of the regular Temple service. But they are also intended to remind us of the light of our holy religion, which Antiochus Epiphanes attempted in vain to extinguish; it again shed forth its light, and shone brighter and brighter every successive day.

Purim.

פּוּרִים or "*Feast of Lots*," is celebrated on the 14*th of Adar (the Second Adar in a leap-year), in commemoration of the defeat of Haman's wicked plans. Haman was chief minister to Ahasuerus, king of Persia, and planned to kill all the Jews in the Persian Empire, but the Almighty frustrated his designs through the agency of* MORDECAI *and his cousin* ESTHER. *The feast is called* PURIM, *that is,* "*lots," because Haman had cast lots in order to find out the day most favourable to his plans.*

We celebrate Purim—

(1) By reading the book of Esther, which contains the history of Haman's wicked plans and their frustration.

(2) By giving presents to our friends, מִשְׁלוֹחַ מָנוֹת and gifts to the poor (מַתָּנוֹת לָאֶבְיוֹנִים).

(3) By a festive meal (סְעוּדַת פּוּרִים).

The 13th of Adar, being the day appointed for the slaughter of the Jews, is now kept as a fast-day, and is called תַּעֲנִית אֶסְתֵּר, "the Fast of Esther."

The 15th of Adar is called Shushan-Purim, because the Jews in Shushan continued to fight against the enemy on the 14th, and kept the feast on the 15th.

The Four Fasts.

There are four days kept as fast-days in commemoration of events connected with the fall of Jerusalem. They are called in the Bible (Zech. viii. 19) *the fast of the fourth month, and the fast of the fifth, and the fast* of the seventh, and the fast of the tenth. These days are the anniversaries of the commencement of the siege of Jerusalem (10th of Tebeth), of the breach made in the wall (17th of Tammuz), of the destruction of the Temple (9th of Ab), and of the murder of Gedaliah (3rd of Tishri). The 9th of Ab is kept as a day of fasting and mourning for the destruction of the Temple. According to tradition, both the first and the second Temple were destroyed on the same day.

NOTE 1.—These fasts begin with daybreak, except the fast of the 9th of Ab, which commences with the previous evening and lasts twenty-four hours. During the day the Lamentations of Jeremiah, various elegies called קִינוֹת "Lamentations," and the Book of Job are read.

NOTE 2.—The Sabbath preceding the fast of Ab is called שַׁבַּת חָזוֹן and the Sabbath following שַׁבַּת נַחֲמוּ because the Haphtaroth on these Sabbaths (ch. i. and ch. xl. of Isaiah) begin respectively with the words חָזוֹן and נַחֲמוּ; the one containing rebukes and threats, the other a message of comfort.

TEXTS OF MORAL DUTIES.

(FOR STANDARD III.)

Love of God.—" Thou shalt love the Lord thy God with all thine heart, and with all thy soul, and with all thy might" (Deut. vi. 5).

Love of our fellow-men.—" Thou shalt love thy neighbour as thyself: I am the Lord" (Lev. xix. 18).

(*a.*) The love shown in our conduct towards those who have wronged or offended us:—

"Thou shalt not hate thy brother in thine heart: thou shalt in any wise rebuke thy brother and not suffer sin upon him" (*Ibid.* 17).

"Thou shalt not avenge nor bear any grudge against the children of thy people" (*Ibid.* 18).

(*b.*) In our conduct toward those who are in need of help and sympathy:—

"Thou shalt not oppress a stranger; for ye know the heart of a stranger, for ye were strangers in the land of Egypt: I am the Lord your God" (Exod. xxiii. 9).

"If a stranger sojourn with thee in your land, ye shall not vex him. But the stranger that dwelleth with you shall be unto you as one born among you; and thou shalt love him as thyself; for ye were strangers in the land of Egypt: I am the Lord your God" (Lev. xix. 33–34).

"Ye shall not afflict any widow or fatherless child" (Exod. xxii. 22).

"Thou shalt not defraud an hired servant that is poor and needy, whether he be of thy brethren, or of thy strangers that are in thy land within thy gates" (Deut. xxiv. 14).

"Thou shalt open thine hand wide unto thy brother, to thy poor, and to thy needy, in thy land" (*Ibid.* xv. 11).

"If thou lend money to any of my people that is poor by thee, thou shalt not be to him as a creditor, neither shalt thou lay upon him usury" (Exod. xxii. 25).

(*c.*) In our conduct toward the old:—

"Thou shalt rise up before the hoary head, and honour the face of the old man, and fear thy God: I am the Lord" (Lev. xix. 32).

Personal Holiness.—"Ye shall be holy: for I the Lord your God am holy" (Lev. xix. 2).

(*a.*) Holiness shown in abstaining from acts and words that would degrade and disgrace us, such as dishonesty or slander:—

"Ye shall not steal, neither deal falsely, neither lie one to another" (Lev. xix. 11).

"Ye shall do no unrighteousness in judgment, in meteyard, in weight, or in measure" (*Ibid.* 35).

"If you sell ought unto thy neighbour, or buyest ought of thy neighbour's hand, ye shall not oppress one another" (*Ibid.* xxv. 14).

"Thou shalt not go up and down as a tale-bearer among thy people" (Lev. xix. 16).

"Keep thy tongue from evil, and thy lips from speaking guile" (Ps. xxxiv. 11).

(b.) In seeking to improve and to do what is right and noble :—

"Wash you, make you clean ; put away the evil of your doings from before mine eyes ; cease to do evil ; learn to do well" (Is. i. 16, 17).

"He hath showed thee, O man, what is good ; and what doth the Lord require of thee, but to do justly, and to love mercy, and to walk humbly with thy God ?" (Micah vi. 8).

THE THIRTEEN PRINCIPLES OF FAITH.

שְׁלשׁ עֶשְׂרֵה עִקָּרִים

(FOR STANDARDS IV. AND VI.)

The Thirteen Principles are divided into three groups:—
1. *The first five speak of God,* מְצִיאוּת הַבּוֹרֵא
2. *The next four speak of Divine Revelation,* תּוֹרָה מִן הַשָּׁמַיִם
3. *The last four speak of Divine Providence and Justice,* שָׂכָר וְעֹנֶשׁ

THE FIRST GROUP OF PRINCIPLES.

God and His Attributes.

The belief in God is the foundation of all religion. Belief in God is the conviction that there exists a Being who is the Creator and Ruler of the whole universe, to whom we are responsible for all our deeds, words, and thoughts. This Being we call God. We do not see Him; we cannot form any definite notion or image of Him, for He is beyond all human imagination and conception. We know Him from His works and His words.

NOTE 1.—We notice that for everything in existence there is a cause that produced it; that cause, again, owes its existence to another cause, and so on. There must, therefore, have been a

First Cause—God, who is the source of all causes, the Creator of all things.

NOTE 2.—We look at the grandeur of nature as displayed in high mountains, mighty rivers, large seas, the heavenly luminaries, &c., and we exclaim, "The heavens tell the glory of God, and the expanse declareth the work of His hand" (Ps. xix. 2); "How great are Thy works, O Lord! exceeding deep are Thy plans" (xcii. 6). Comp. Ps. civ. 24.

NOTE 3.—Not only in these grand things, but even in the smallest creature a wise and omnipotent Creator is recognised. Everywhere in nature we find order and regularity and evidence of the wisdom and the power of the Creator.

NOTE 4.—In the history of nations as well as of individuals, in the rise and fall of empires, in the good and in the evil fortunes of men, the working may be traced of the mighty though invisible hand of the Supreme Ruler.

NOTE 5.—In our own hearts there is a certain inborn notion of an invisible force that rules the universe. Such a notion is found among almost all nations of the earth.

NOTE 6.—The Divine messages communicated to us through His Prophets inform us about God, His existence and His attributes.

The First Principle.

"*I firmly believe that God is the Creator and Ruler of all creatures, and that He alone was, is, and will be the Maker of everything.*"

The first lesson which the Bible teaches us is: "In the beginning God created the heavens and the earth" (Gen. i. 1). There was a time when the earth upon which we live, the heavens with all the suns, moons, and stars, did not exist: all these had a beginning at a certain time, when the Will of God brought them into existence. "He spake, and it was done; He commanded, and it stood fast" (Ps. xxxiii. 9).

NOTE.—It is true we perceive the action of certain natural forces and laws, and connect them with the phenomena noticed by us.

The part that such forces as light, heat, electricity, magnetism, gravitation, and the like play in nature is appointed to them by the Will of the Creator. When we say this or that has been produced by light, heat, &c., we are correct in so far as the direct cause is concerned, but it is God who directs these forces. Or when we notice things, individuals, or species produced and developed according to the law of evolution, this law is dependent on the Divine Will. This principle is expressed in the first creed by the words, "And He alone was, is, and will be the Maker of everything." This is the meaning of the words: "He who renews constantly every day the work of the Creation" (Daily Prayers, Morning Service).

The Attributes of God.

The following are the attributes of God expressed in the first group of Principles: Unity, Incorporeality, Eternity, and Omnipotence.

The Second Principle—The Unity of God.

"*I firmly believe that the Creator is One; that there is no Unity like unto His in any way; and that He alone was, is, and will be our God.*"

The Unity of God is frequently taught in the Bible. We repeat thrice daily: "Hear, O Israel: the Lord is our God, the Lord is One" (Deut. vi. 4). It is for this belief that Jews have willingly sacrificed their life; for this belief they have suffered, and are still suffering, martyrdom of all kinds; this belief distinguishes our faith from that of other nations, but we see it gradually spreading, and hope to see it accepted by all mankind.

The words "There is no Unity like unto His" have this meaning: We say of many a thing that it is one;

we speak of one man, one house, &c., well knowing that there are other men, other houses, &c. But when we speak of *One God*, we rigidly exclude the existence of another God. Besides, one man, one house, &c., though being one, form a compound of several elements. This is not the case with God.

The words, " And He alone was, is, and will be our God," express our belief that there has never been, and there never will be, any other being with the divine attributes before mentioned, such as, *e.g.*, has been assumed by Christians.

Third Principle—Incorporeality.

"*I firmly believe that God is Incorporeal, that He has not any corporeal qualities, and that nothing can be compared unto Him.*"

God's Incorporeality is inseparable from His Unity, because a corporeal thing cannot be truly one and simple. Every corporeal thing consists of various elements, has different dimensions, &c. But God is Incorporeal. We cannot ascribe to Him length, breadth, or height; He has no shape, and is not limited, like a body, by lines or surfaces; His existence does not depend, like that of bodies, on certain conditions and circumstances, and is, therefore, unlimited in time and space.

NOTE.—If, nevertheless, in the Bible and in our prayers expressions occur like " hand," " foot," " finger," " voice," &c., of God, or " He went," " He descended," &c., expressions which imply a corporeal form, we have to understand them in a figurative sense. Such terms are called *anthropomorphisms;* that is, terms borrowed from the qualities and the actions of man, and applied figuratively, in a spiritual sense, to God. We are more accustomed to corporeal things, and we understand abstract ideas more easily by comparing them to corporeal things and figuratively expressing them in terms proper to the latter. In reality, however, God cannot be compared to His creatures. "To whom then will ye liken God? and what likeness will you compare unto Him?" (Isa. xl. 18).

The Incorporeality of God necessarily implies *Omnipresence* and *Omniscience*. God is everywhere, sees and knows everything. "Can any hide himself in secret places that I shall not see him? saith the Lord" (Jer. xxiii. 24). "Whither shall I go from thy spirit? or whither shall I flee from thy presence? If I ascend up into heaven, thou art there; if I make my bed in the grave, behold, thou art there. If I take the wings of the morning, and dwell in the uttermost part of the sea, even there shall thy hand lead me, and thy right hand shall hold me. If I say, Surely the darkness shall overwhelm me, and the light about me shall be night: even the darkness hideth not from thee, but the night shineth as the day: the darkness and the light are both alike to thee" (Ps. cxxxix. 8-13).

Fourth Principle—Eternity

"*I firmly believe that God was the first, and will be the last.*"

"Thy years are throughout all generations; of old hast Thou laid the foundations of the earth, and the heavens are the work of Thy hands. They shall perish, but Thou shalt endure: yea, all of them shall wax old like a garment: as a vesture shalt Thou change them, and they shall be changed: but Thou art the same, and Thy years shall have no end" (Ps. cii. 24–27).

Fifth Principle—Omnipotence.

"*I firmly believe that it is God alone to whom we ought to pray, and that no other being ought to be addressed in prayer.*"

God is Omnipotent or Almighty : He can do everything, whilst any other being can only do as much as he is empowered by the Almighty to do. Nothing can do us good or harm if the Lord has not ordained it. He alone can fulfil our wishes, can save us from danger, can frustrate the schemes of our enemies and give our friends the means of assisting us. He alone, therefore, should be addressed in prayer ; to pray to any other being is useless and senseless. " Are there any among the vanities of the heathen that can cause rain ? or can the heavens give showers ? Art not thou he (that causeth rain, that giveth showers), O Lord our God ? " (Jer. xiv. 22). To God alone we pray, in Him alone we trust ; for He hath both the power and the will to do us good.

NOTE.—In addition to the above attributes there are others which frequently occur in the Bible and in the Prayer-book. The most important of them are : Kindness and Goodness, Justice, Holiness, and Perfection.

Kindness and Goodness.

God is all-kind, all-good. " God is good to all, and His mercy is over all His works" (Ps. cxlv. 9). The ways of God's goodness are manifold, and in our prayers we speak of God's thirteen attributes of goodness, שְׁלשׁ עֶשְׂרֵה מִדּוֹת viz., " The Lord, the Lord is mighty, merciful and gracious, slow to anger and abounding in loving-kindness and truth ; keeping loving-kindness for thousands, forgiving iniquity and transgression and sin, and that will by no means clear the guilty ; visiting the iniquity of the fathers upon the children, and upon the children's children, upon the third and upon the fourth generation " (Exod. xxxiv. 6, 7).

Justice.

"The Rock, perfect is his work, for all his ways are just ; a God of faithfulness is he, and of no iniquity, just and right is he" (Deut. xxxii. 4). "God is just in all his ways, and kind in all his works" (Ps. cxlv. 17). If in some instances the divine gifts seem to our judgment to be distributed unjustly, we must bear in mind that our knowledge is imperfect; we frequently mistake reward for punishment, and punishment for reward, and judge our neighbour more according to appearance than according to his true merits. (See Eleventh Principle.)

Holiness and Perfection.

We ascribe to God everything good and noble in the highest and most perfect degree. He is holy and His name is holy; His name excludes everything unholy, common, and base.

"For Thou art not a God that delighteth in injustice; evil doth not dwell with Thee" (Ps. v. 5). "Holy, holy, holy, is the Lord of hosts: His glory filleth the whole earth" (Isa. vi. 3).

THE SECOND GROUP OF PRINCIPLES.

Revelation and Prophecy.

A *prophet*, נָבִיא is a person who has received a divine communication and the charge to communicate it to his fellow-men. He has no other knowledge of the future but that revealed to him by God. In other things his knowledge is human and natural, such as is accessible to all. The process by which the prophets learn the Will of God is called *Inspiration*, and the prophet is *an inspired man;* that is, a man endowed with *the Spirit of the Lord.* The prophets were also *holy men;* their mind was filled with pure thoughts, their deeds were noble, and their conduct blameless. They were *men of God*, or *servants of the Lord*, because their life was wholly devoted to the service of the Lord. They were trustworthy men, and all their words are true.

NOTE 1.—Both the Hebrew נָבִיא and the English "prophet" signify originally "speaker" (comp. Exod. vii. 1).

NOTE 2.—There were also inspired men who had no message for their fellow-men, and were not prophets. But the Spirit of the Lord that filled them impelled them to extraordinary deeds, or guided them in the production of useful and instructive books, or in their judgment upon good and evil, truth and falsehood.

Prophets were: *e.g.*, Moses, Samuel, Nathan, Elijah, Elisha, Isaiah, Jeremiah, &c. Inspired men: *e.g.*, the Patriarchs, Joshua, the Judges, David, Solomon, Daniel, and the men that fixed the Canon of the Holy Writings, *i.e.*, decided which were the books that were written by Divine authority and contain the message of God to man.

The prophets were not all alike; they had different degrees of prophetic inspiration. As we, who are not prophets, cannot fully understand the real nature and method of prophecy, so we are unable to obtain a clear notion of the differences between one prophet and the other. We only know that Moses was the greatest prophet, and whilst other prophets received Divine messages with regard to occasional events, the word of God revealed to Moses contained permanent laws, "statutes for ever throughout all generations." The Divine messages of the prophets are contained in the Holy Writings.[1]

However different the degrees of prophetic inspiration were with which the prophets were favoured, one thing was common to all of them; their words were true, and this is expressed in the sixth principle, as follows:—

Sixth Principle.

"*I firmly believe that all the words of the prophets are true.*"

Seventh Principle.

"*I firmly believe that the prophecy of our Teacher Moses was a prophecy in the truest sense of the word,*

---

[1] See Appendix II.

and that he was the chief of all prophets, both of those before him and those after him."

The distinction between Moses and other prophets is expressed in the following words addressed by the Almighty to Aaron and Miriam: "If there be among you a prophet of the Lord, I make myself known unto him in a vision, in a dream I speak with him. Not so my servant Moses; he is faithful in all my house. Mouth to mouth I speak with him, even manifestly, and not in dark speeches, and he beholds the similitude of the Lord" (Num. xii. 6–8). It is further stated in the Pentateuch: "There did not rise again a prophet like unto Moses, whom the Lord knew face to face" (Deut. xxxiv. 9).

Eighth Principle.

"*I firmly believe that the Torah, at present in our hand, is the same that was given to our Teacher Moses, peace be with him!*"

The Torah has not undergone any change. It was anxiously guarded by the nation as a holy treasure. It was not the property of a class or caste, but belonged to all. Even in periods of corruption and idolatry there were men who remained faithful to the Law, knew it thoroughly, and would have easily detected any alteration, if any person had dared to tamper with the Holy Treasure.

Ninth Principle.

"*I firmly believe that this Law will not be changed, and that no other Law will be revealed by the Creator, blessed be His name.*"

This principle is the expression of our belief in the immutability of the Torah. God, the Immutable, gave us also an immutable Law. All the prophets exhorted the Israelites to remain faithful to the Law, and the last of the prophets says in the name of God: "Remember the Law of Moses, my servant" (Mal. iii. 12).

NOTE.—The belief in the immutability of the divine Law led our forefathers to reject Christianity and Islamism, both of which are based on a pretended revelation contrary to the Law of Moses.

The immutability of the divine Law is also a test of the truthfulness of a prophet: if he teaches anything contrary to the teaching of the Law he is a false prophet, in spite of whatever wonderful things he might be able to accomplish. "And thou shalt stone him, that he die, because he hath sought to draw thee away from the Lord thy God" (Deut. xiii. 11).

THE THIRD GROUP OF PRINCIPLES.

Providence and Justice.

The first five Principles having expressed our belief in God, His Unity, Incorporeality, Eternity, and Omnipotence, and the next four our belief in the fact that the Almighty has made His Will known to mankind through the prophets, the remaining Principles refer to the consequences of man's obedience or disobedience to the Will of his Creator.

Tenth Principle.

"*I firmly believe, that God knows all the deeds of the sons of men, and all their thoughts; as it is said, 'He who hath formed their hearts altogether, He knoweth all their deeds'*" (Ps. xxxiii. 15).

Some believe that it is beneath the dignity of God to take notice of man's doings. The verse from the Psalms has therefore been added here as an argument, viz., if it was not beneath the dignity of God to create man and to form his heart, it cannot be beneath His dignity to watch him, and to take notice of his actions, his words, and his thoughts. "The great, the mighty God, the Lord of hosts is His name; great in counsel, and mighty in work: whose eyes are open upon all the ways of the sons of men" (Jer. xxxii. 19).

Eleventh Principle.

"*I firmly believe that God rewards those who keep His commandments, and punishes those who transgress His commandments.*"

Although the mere consciousness that whatsoever we do is seen and noticed by our All-kind, All-wise, and Almighty Father is our best reward and encouragement when we do something good, and our severest punishment when we do anything wrong, we are taught by the Word of God that other kinds of reward and punishment await us. The Bible contains many events illustrating this principle, and in fact it is the principal object of the writers of the history in the Bible to inculcate the lesson that God rewards and punishes man according as he deserves. "If ye be willing and obedient, ye shall eat the good of the land: but if ye refuse and rebel, ye shall be devoured with the sword: for the mouth of the Lord hath spoken it" (Isa. i. 19, 20).

Twelfth Principle—Messiah מָשִׁיחַ.

"*I firmly believe that the Anointed* (הַמָּשִׁיחַ) *will come; and although He tarries, I wait nevertheless every day for His coming.*"

The Israelites were chosen by God to be "a kingdom of priests and a holy nation" (Exod. xix. 6). As a kingdom of priests they had to spread the knowledge and the worship of God; as a holy nation they were expected to become an example of goodness and righteousness to all people. Palestine was given to them as inheritance, and Zion or Jerusalem was their religious centre: "For out of Zion shall go forth instruction, and the word of the Lord from Jerusalem" (Isa. ii. 3).

The sins of Israel have brought about the loss of their independence as a nation, of their land and Temple, that is, their national as well as their religious centre. But the Divine decree that ordered the exile of our nation has also promised the restoration of Israel, when by love of God, by an earnest desire to fulfil His commandments, and by leading a virtuous and holy life, the Israelites will make themselves worthy of this Divine blessing. A descendant of the house of David, a human being, and not any more of Divine descent than any other man, will then be anointed [1]

---

[1] It was in ancient times the custom to anoint persons when appointed to important offices, such as kings, priests, and prophets. "Anointed" became, therefore, in Hebrew identical with "appointed." Cyrus, *e.g.*, was "anointed" to conquer Babylon and liberate the captive Jews. The Israelites are the "anointed of the Lord" to teach all mankind by their own good example the true faith and the true worship of God.

(מָשִׁיחַ) to be at the head of our nation, and a source of peace and happiness to all mankind.

Note.—By the Messianic time or "the days of the anointed" (יְמוֹת הַמָּשִׁיחַ), the chief of our national hopes, we mean (1) the days of the restoration of Israel to the Holy Land, the rebuilding of the Temple in Jerusalem, the resumption of the Divine Service therein, and the return of the Divine Glory (שְׁכִינָה) to Zion; (2) the days of universal cessation of warfare, and the highest development of all human virtues and happiness.

The characteristics of the Messianic days are given by the prophets as follows:—"And it shall come to pass in the latter days, that the mountain of the Lord's house shall be established in the top of the mountains, and shall be exalted above the hills; and all nations shall flow unto it. And many people shall go and say, Come ye, and let us go up to the mountain of the Lord, to the house of the God of Jacob; and He will teach us of His ways, and we will walk in His paths: for out of Zion shall go forth the law, and the word of the Lord from Jerusalem. And He shall judge between the nations and shall decide for many peoples: and they shall beat their swords into ploughshares, and their spears into pruning-hooks: nation shall not lift up sword against nation, neither shall they learn war any more" (Isa. ii. 2-4).

"And the wolf shall dwell with the lamb, and the leopard shall lie down with the kid: and the calf and the young lion and the fatling together, and a little child shall lead them. And the cow and the bear shall feed: their young ones shall lie down together; and the lion shall eat straw like the ox. And the sucking child shall play on the hole of the asp, and the weaned child shall put his hand on the cockatrice's den. They shall not hurt nor destroy in all my holy mountain: for the earth shall be full of the knowledge of the Lord, as the waters cover the sea" (*Ibid.* xi. 6-9).

"On that day shall the Lord be One, and His name One" (Jer. xiv. 9).

"Then will I turn to the peoples a pure language that they may all call upon the name of the Lord, to serve Him with one consent" (Zeph. iii. 9).

At various times men have come forward as Messiah or prophet;

but they satisfied neither the conditions of Messiah nor those of a true prophet. We therefore continue in our hope and in our faith that the word of God spoken by His prophets "shall not return unto Him void, but it shall accomplish that which He pleaseth, and it shall prosper in the thing whereto He sent it" (Isa. lv. 11), that the promised Messiah will come, and with him the blessings of the Messianic time.

Thirteenth Principle—Future Life.

" I firmly believe that there will be a resurrection of the dead, at the time when it shall please the Creator, blessed be His name!"

Note.—The enjoyment and the loss of life, health, wealth, and honour are frequently mentioned in the Bible as reward and punishment for good and bad conduct respectively. Life, health, wealth, and honour are intelligible to the multitude; they are most hoped for, and their loss most feared. They form the basis of the prosperity of a nation, and as in the Bible the Israelites are generally addressed as a nation, it is natural that the acquisition of these blessings should form the reward of the Israelites for obedience to the word of God, their loss the punishment for disobedience.

But for the individual the possession of these advantages, however pleasant, is no real blessing, no true happiness. Short is the time during which the individual can enjoy these gifts; they do not follow him in death, and are sometimes the source of grief and misery. "Riches are sometimes kept by the owner thereof to his hurt" (Eccles. v. 13). A better and a lasting reward our just and kind Father has prepared for those of His children who love Him truly and obey His commandments.

Our existence does not end with death. Two elements are contained in man—body and soul. The soul is the nobler and the better element. It is the soul that makes man an image of God, and gives him superiority over the rest of the creation. In death the body returns to the earth whence it came, and the soul returns to God who put it into the body (Eccles. xii. 7).

NOTE.—The soul of man is not of the same nature as the soul of other living beings; the latter is merely their vital faculty, and comes to an end with the body. We need only carefully read the history of the Creation, and we shall see that the soul of man is "the breath of life" נִשְׁמַת חַיִּים which He breathed into man's nostrils, and this "breath of the Almighty" is immortal. After man's death, which is merely a separation of body and soul, the elements which, united, form his life, the body returns to the earth, and resolves itself into its various parts, but the soul continues to live for ever. The life of the soul in the separate state is called "future life" or "the world to come" הָעוֹלָם הַבָּא. It is the life in which, as our Sages say, "there is no eating or drinking, or any other of earthly enjoyments, but the enjoyment of continually beholding the splendour of the Divine glory." There the righteous receive the true reward, and the wicked the true punishment; and what a terrible punishment it must be to be excluded from the presence of the Divine glory even for a moment! Such a moment of agony is not compensated for by all the pleasures of the earth! For "better is one moment of bliss in the future life earned by good deeds than all earthly happiness" (Aboth iv. 18). But the consciousness of having accomplished a good deed is the greatest happiness, for "one moment of improvement and good deeds here on earth outweighs all the enjoyment of the future life" (*Ibid.*).

We cannot correctly picture to ourselves the enjoyment or the nature of the future life. What we read of it in Talmud, Midrash, and other books must be taken in a figurative sense. We speak figuratively of the גַּן עֵדֶן Garden of Eden or Paradise, as the future abode of the good; of גֵּיא הִנּוֹם the valley of Hinnom (hell), as the future abode of the wicked, because these names are suggestive of the greatest possible pleasure and the greatest possible pain.

The soul of man continues to live after its separation from the body; new life is thus given to man after his death, and the transition into the new life is called תְּחִיַת הַמֵּתִים Revival or Resurrection of the dead. Whether the soul will enjoy a second life on earth united with the body, and if so, how and when this reunion will take place, is unknown to us. We feel convinced that there will be a second life after the life here on earth is completed, but we are unable to clearly define or describe that life.

The belief that the soul continues to live after man's death is also called the belief in the Immortality of the Soul.

"My flesh and my heart faileth, but God shall be the strength of my heart and my portion for ever" (Ps. lxxiii. 26).

"And after my skin, when this body is destroyed, and when my flesh is gone, I shall see God" (Job xix. 26).

"As for me, I will behold thy face in righteousness: I shall be satisfied with thy likeness" (Ps. xvii. 15).

DIVINE WORSHIP.

(STANDARD IV.)

"YE shall serve the Lord your God." Prayer[1] is one of the many ways of serving the Lord. We call it Divine Service. We may pray to God and pour out our heart before the Almighty all day long in any way or in any language we choose. The merit of prayer does not lie in what we utter, but in the feelings that occupy our heart while we pray.

Our Sages have expressed this principle in the following way:—

"Better a little with devotion (כַּוָּנָה) than much without devotion."

"Prayer without devotion is like a body without the soul."

"During prayer bear in mind before whom thou standest: before the King of the kings of kings, the Holy One, Blessed be He!"

Decorous conduct is an essential of genuine prayer. Its absence during our prayer shows that we are not

---

[1] The Hebrew תְּפִלָּה "prayer," is derived from פלל "to judge," and originally signifies "judgment." The name תְּפִלָּה therefore implies that before we approach God with our petition we ought to try ourselves and judge whether we have purified our heart from everything that would make us unworthy of addressing the Most Holy.

thinking of the All-holy Being to whom our words are spoken, or that we feel no respect for Him.

Our direct object in praying to God is to commune with Him, to give expression to our feelings of reverence and gratitude, and to ask for His blessings. One of the chief effects of prayer, however, is the elevation of our thoughts, the purification of our heart, and the improvement of our conduct.

NOTE.—In order to foster a disposition for devotion and facilitate its expression, it was necessary to fix to some extent the time, the form, and the contents of the prayer, without, however, restraining the free effusion of the heart before our Heavenly Father. Such rules are especially necessary for תְּפִלָּה בְּצִבּוּר "public Divine worship."

Although we constantly enjoy the blessings of God, the very breath we breathe being the gift of our Heavenly Father, certain seasons of the day, of the week, of the month, and of the year, and certain occasions and events, have been selected as especially fit for reminding us of God's kindness and predisposing our heart to devotion. In the day, the beginning, the middle, and the end, or morning, afternoon, and evening have been selected; in the week, Sabbath; in the month, New-moon; in the year, the Festivals. To these must be added all occasions on which we experience a special feeling of pleasure or grief.

Our prayers are therefore divided into (1) prayers at fixed times, and (2) occasional prayers.

1. *Prayers at Fixed Times.*

"In the evening, and in the morning, and at noon I meditate and cry, and He hears my voice" (Ps. lv. 18). We read of Daniel that he prayed to God three times every day (Dan. vi. 10). These daily prayers are accordingly called: מַעֲרִיב Evening-prayer; שַׁחֲרִית Morning-prayer, and מִנְחָה Afternoon-prayer. On

Sabbath, New-moon, and Festivals an "additional prayer" מוּסָף is inserted between the Morning and the Afternoon Services; and on the Day of Atonement we have a fifth prayer נְעִילָה "conclusion," after מִנְחָה.

The term תְּפִלָּה "prayer," in its wider sense includes: (1.) Prayer in its proper sense: petition. (2.) Praises. (3.) Thanksgiving. (4.) Meditations on God and on our duties. (5.) Confessions. (6.) Readings from Biblical and post-Biblical sacred literature. תְּפִלָּה is used in a narrower sense of the *Amidah* (prayer offered up while standing) or *Shemonah-esre* (Eighteen Benedictions).

The chief sections of our daily prayer are שְׁמַע and שְׁמוֹנֶה עֶשְׂרֵה.

The Reading of Shema, קְרִיאַת שְׁמַע.

In obedience to the precept, "Thou shalt speak of them—*i.e.*, "the words which I command thee this day"—when thou liest down and when thou riseth," three sections of the Torah are read daily in the morning and in the evening, viz., (1) Deut. vi. 4–9, beginning שְׁמַע "hear;" (2) *Ibid.* xi. 13–21, beginning וְהָיָה אִם שָׁמֹעַ "If ye will diligently hearken;" (3) Num. xv. 37–41, beginning וַיֹּאמֶר "And he said." The first section, שְׁמַע teaches the Unity of God, and our duty to love this One God with all our heart, to make His Word the subject of our constant meditation, and to instil it into the heart of the young.

The second section, וְהָיָה אִם שָׁמֹעַ, contains the lesson of reward and punishment: that our success depends on our obedience to the Will of God. This important truth must constantly be kept before our eyes and the eyes of our children.

The third section, וַיֹּאמֶר contains the commandment of צִיצִת "fringe," the object of which is to remind us of God's precepts: "Ye shall see it, and remember all the commandments of the Lord and do them, and that ye seek not after your own heart and your own eyes, after which ye use to go astray, that ye remember and do all my commandments, and be holy unto your God."

The reading of *Shema* is preceded by two בְּרָכוֹת (1.) Praise of the Creator for the regular sequence of day and night, light and darkness. (2.) Praise of His goodness in giving us the Torah, and prayer for His assistance in the study of the Torah. The *Shema* is followed by a reflection on the last words of the third section, "I am the Lord your God," and an expression of our faith in the truth of these words, which imply that God will in future redeem Israel.

In the evening this blessing is followed by another containing a prayer for protection during the night.

The Eighteen Benedictions, שְׁמוֹנֶה עֶשְׂרֵה or עֲמִידָה

This prayer contained originally eighteen paragraphs, compiled and arranged by the men of the Great Synagogue אַנְשֵׁי כְנֶסֶת הַגְּדוֹלָה. Later on, when attempts were made by evil-minded persons to frustrate the national hopes of the Messianic time, the nineteenth paragraph (וְלַמַּלְשִׁינִים) was added, praying for the defeat of the schemes of these men.

NOTE.—The first three paragraphs contain praise of God's goodness to us, the descendants of the pious patriarchs (1), His omnipotence (2), His holiness (3).

TEXT-BOOK OF THE JEWISH RELIGION. 57

The next thirteen paragraphs are petitions for our individual and national well-being; for our individual well-being (4–9): for reason and wisdom (4), assistance in our endeavour to return to God (5), forgiveness of our sins (6), deliverance from trouble (7), from illness (8), and from want (9).

For our national well-being (10–15): for bringing together those who are scattered (10), under good leaders (11), protected from the evil designs of opponents (12); for support of the faithful (13), rebuilding of Jerusalem (14), and the advent of Messiah (15).

The sixteenth paragraph is a prayer that our petition may be accepted (16).

The last three paragraphs include a petition for the re-establishment of Divine Service in the Temple of Jerusalem (17), thanksgiving (18), and prayer for peace and prosperity (19).

Having finished our prayer, we express our wish that our lips, from which prayer to God has come forth, may not be defiled by unworthy language.

On Sabbath, Holy days, and Musaph of New-moon the thirteen middle paragraphs are replaced by one; in Musaph of New-year by three.

Morning Service, שַׁחֲרִית

Besides *Shema* and *Amidah* the service contains: (1) בִּרְכוֹת הַשַּׁחַר "Blessings of the morning," referring to the change from night to day, from sleep to fresh life, from rest to activity; (2) Sacrifices: passages from the Bible and post-Biblical writings referring to the daily sacrificial service; (3.) פְּסוּקֵי or מִזְמוֹרִים דְזִמְרָא Psalms, and the Song of Moses; (4) תַּחֲנוּנִים Supplications of various kinds; the whole concluding with (5) Thanksgiving for the privilege of proclaiming the Unity of God, and the expression of our hope to see the worship of the One God adopted by all mankind. This prayer, beginning with the words עָלֵינוּ לְשַׁבֵּחַ "it is our duty to praise," is called עָלֵינוּ.

On Mondays, Thursdays, New-moon day, Sabbath, and Festivals Readings from the Law (קְרִיאַת הַתּוֹרָה) form part of the Service.

The prayer for the establishment of the general worship of the One God is also contained in the *Kaddish* קַדִּישׁ "sanctification," recited in various forms in Synagogue by the Reader, and also by Mourners. The latter recite it in order to express their faith in God and resignation to His Will.

Additional Service, מוּסָף

On Sabbath, New-moon, and Holy days the second part of the Morning Service is called מוּסָף "Additional Service," the essential parts of which are the *Amidah, Alenu,* and *Kaddish.*

Afternoon Service, מִנְחָה and נְעִילָה

The chief parts of this service are Ps. cxlv., *Amidah,* Supplications (תַּחֲנוּן), *Alenu,* and *Kaddish. Neïlah* on the Day of Atonement consists chiefly of the *Amidah.*

Evening Prayer, מַעֲרִיב

This service consists of *Shema, Amidah, Alenu,* and *Kaddish.* In some congregations a few psalms are added. In the house of mourning Ps. xlix. or xvi. is recited.

NOTE 1.—Additions are sometimes made to the ordinary prayers: (1.) *Selichoth,* prayers for forgiveness, on fast-days, penitential days, and in the month of Ellul. (2.) *Piyyutim,* poetical compositions added on Festivals and certain Sabbaths. (3.) *Maaraboth,* poetical compositions added to the Evening Prayer.

NOTE 2.—These services are read either in Synagogue or at home. In addition to these there is a Night-prayer said at home before retiring to rest; the essential element in it is the first portion of *Shema,* and it is called קְרִיאַת שְׁמַע שֶׁעַל הַמִּטָּה reading of *Shema* before going to bed.

2. Occasional Prayers. Benedictions, בְּרָכוֹת

The feeling of our dependence on the goodness of God must constantly be present to our mind. Whatever we enjoy, whether it be eating or drinking, or some pleasing or remarkable sight, an agreeable smell, a festivity on a joyful event, or the performance of a Divine commandment (מִצְוָה); whatever befall us, whether it be pleasant or unpleasant—all this we consider as sent to us by the Will of the Almighty, and we express our conviction by a suitable blessing, בְּרָכָה. There is the general rule: It is unlawful for man to enjoy anything on earth without previously acknowledging by a בְּרָכָה that God is the source whence the enjoyment is derived. For different cases different forms of the בְּרָכָה have been fixed.[1]

Grace, בִּרְכַּת הַמָּזוֹן

One of the most important of these benedictions is the prayer after meals, בִּרְכַּת הַמָּזוֹן "the benediction for food," or Grace. It is also called "the three benedictions," שָׁלֹשׁ בְּרָכוֹת because originally it consisted of three benedictions: (1) Praise of God's providential care of all creatures: בִּרְכַּת הַזָּן; (2) thanks for our food, as well as for our national gifts, Palestine, the Covenant, and the Law: הוֹדָאָה "thanksgiving," or בִּרְכַּת הָאָרֶץ "blessing for the land;" (3) prayer for the restoration of Zion and the rebuilding of the Temple: בִּנְיַן יְרוּשָׁלַיִם.

In the course of time a fourth blessing was added (הַטּוֹב וְהַמֵּטִיב) in commemoration of the relief given to the Jews after the close of the war with Hadrian. On special occasions, such as weddings and the like, appropriate additions are made.

When three grown-up male persons or more have their meal together, a special introductory form is used, called זִמּוּן; that is, one of the company acts as reader, and the rest form the congregation.

NOTE.—Before meals we wash our hands, say the blessing עַל נְטִילַת יָדַיִם, and eat a piece of bread, after having said the blessing הַמּוֹצִיא.

---

[1] See Appendix VI.

OUTWARD SIGNS AS REMINDERS OF GOD'S PRESENCE.

(*FOR STANDARDS IV. AND VI.*)

"Set up for thyself signs," in order not to forget those things which ought to be remembered. Although the best reminder of God's presence is the voice that speaks to us from within, out of our conscience, we nevertheless are liable, as human beings, to forget important duties in the absence of an outward reminder. The Law has appointed three such reminders: מְזוּזָה "doorpost-ornament," צִיצִת "fringe," and תְּפִלִּין "ornament."

1. מְזוּזָה *Doorpost-Symbol.*

The *Mezuzah* is a piece of parchment on which the two first paragraphs of *Shema* (Deut. vi. 4–9 and xi. 13–20) are written. The parchment is rolled together, put into a small case, and fixed on the right-hand doorpost. A small opening is left in the case, where the word שַׁדַּי "Almighty," written on the back of the scroll, is visible.

The object of the *mezuzah* is to remind us of the presence of God, of His Unity, Providence, and Omnipotence, both on entering our home and on leaving it; of the all-seeing eye that watches us, and of the Almighty who will one day call us to account for our deeds, words, and thoughts. The *mezuzah* thus serves to sanctify our dwelling and protect it from being polluted by evil deeds.

2. צִיצִת *Fringes.*

"Thou shalt make unto thee fringes upon the four corners of thy garment wherewith thou coverest thyself" (Deut. xx. 12). The object of this commandment is explained in the third portion of *Shema:* "Ye shall look at it and remember all the commandments of the Lord." We fulfil this commandment in two ways: (1.) We wear the whole day a small garment with four corners each of which is provided with צִיצִת [1] It is called טַלִית קָטָן or אַרְבַּע כַּנְפוֹת (2.) During the morning-prayer—on the Day of Atonement all day long—we wear over our garments a טַלִית (scarf), having צִיצִת on its four corners. Before putting on the טַלִית we say a blessing (בְּרָכָה), thanking God for having given us this commandment.

3. תְּפִלִּין *Ornament.*[2]

"Thou shalt bind them as a sign upon thy hand, and they shall be for a frontlet between thine eyes" (Deut. vi. 8). This commandment occurs in almost the same words four times in the Torah, twice in the

---

[1] צִיצִת admits of two meanings, (1) "fringes," (2) "something to look upon."

[2] So called because worn in the morning during תְּפִלָּה "prayers." The name תְּפִלִּין may also be derived from תפל "to join closely," "to attach," and would thus signify an ornament closely attached to the body.

first two portions of the *Shema*, and twice in the first two paragraphs of the 13th chapter of Exodus.

The object of this commandment is to direct our thoughts to God and His goodness, and to impress certain lessons on our mind.

NOTE.—Tradition has acquainted us with the way in which this law is to be carried out. The four paragraphs that make mention of the commandment of the *Tefillin*, viz., 1, קַדֶּשׁ (Exod. xiii. 1-10); 2, וְהָיָה כִּי יְבִיאֲךָ (*Ibid.* 11-16); 3, שְׁמַע (Deut. vi. 4-9); 4, וְהָיָה אִם שָׁמֹעַ (*Ibid.* xi. 13-20), are twice written down on slips of parchment; each set is put into a leather case (בַּיִת) and by means of leather straps (רְצוּעוֹת) bound on the arm (תְּפִלִּין שֶׁל יָד) "for a sign," and on the head (תְּפִלִּין שֶׁל רֹאשׁ) "for a memorial." Before putting on the *tefillin* an appropriate blessing is said referring to the commandment of *tefillin*. The lessons of which the *tefillin* are intended to remind us are set forth in the four paragraphs as follows:—

1. The first paragraph teaches that we must, in various ways, express our belief in God as the King and Ruler of the universe. Two laws are mentioned in this paragraph which serve this object—the sanctification of the first-born to the service of the Lord, and the celebration of the Feast of unleavened cakes.

2. The second paragraph reminds us of the wonderful way in which God delivered our forefathers from Egyptian bondage. Remembering this deliverance, we are strengthened in our faith in God in days of trouble; for His ways are not ours, and when *we* do not see any prospect of relief God may be preparing help for us.

3. The third paragraph (שְׁמַע) proclaims the Unity of God, and teaches us to love God and obey Him out of love.

4. The fourth paragraph teaches that Providence deals with men according to their merits, according as each deserves reward or punishment.

We lay the *tefillin* on the arm near the heart, and on the head, and whilst doing so we are reminded of our duty to employ the thoughts that rise in our mind, and the desires of our heart, in the service of the Lord, who gave us the powers of thought and will.

The *tefillin* may thus be considered as an outward *sign* of our inner belief in God : we therefore do not put them on on Sabbaths and Festivals, the very observation of which is itself a sign (א׳ת) of our belief in God, the Creator of the universe.

The laying of the *tefillin* is obligatory for all males from their thirteenth birthday. With the completion of his thirteenth year a boy becomes of age in reference to the fulfilment of all religious duties. He is then called בַּר מִצְוָה (lit., a son of the commandment), a member of the Jewish community, upon whom devolve all such duties as a Jew has to perform. On the Sabbath following that birthday, the *Bar-mitsvah* is called to the Law, either to read a portion of the *Sidra* or to listen to its reading, and publicly acknowledge God as the Giver of the Law. Whether this ceremony and the family festivities connected with it take place or not, the obligations devolving on the *Bar-mitsvah* remain the same.

Signs of God's Covenant.

1. The Covenant of Abraham, בְּרִית מִילָה. God made a covenant with Abraham and said, "Thou shalt keep my covenant, thou and thy seed after thee in their generations. This is my covenant, which ye shall keep, between me and you and thy seed after thee : every male child among you shall be circumcised, when eight days old" (Gen. xvii. 9, 10, 12).

2. Sabbath is likewise "an everlasting covenant," "a sign it is between God and the children of Israel for ever" (Exod. xxxi. 16, 17). See p. 16.

Moral Duties.

A. Duties towards God.

"And now, O Israel, what doth the Lord thy God ask of thee, but to fear the Lord thy God, to walk in all His ways, and to love Him, and to serve the Lord thy God with all thy heart and all thy soul?" (Deut. x. 12).

The fear of God (יראת השם) and *the love of God* (אהבת השם) are the fundamental duties towards God, and are, in fact, the source of all our duties.

1. *The fear of God* is not a fear of punishment. We do not fear God because He has the power to harm and torture us. Our fear of God is a fear of displeasing by our deeds, words, and even by our thoughts, Him who loves us and whom we love.

2. *The love of God* finds expression in our eagerness to do everything that pleases Him, and to abstain from everything that displeases Him, and to sacrifice willingly all we possess, even our life, if the Will of God demands it. Our own wishes and desires must be subordinated to His Will and guided by it.

The fear and the love of God create in our heart a feeling of *reverence*. This is strengthened by reflections on the infinite kindness, wisdom, and power displayed in His works. Reverence of God finds an outward expression in the manner we speak of Him and of everything connected with His name; in the manner we behave in the House of God, or during Divine Worship, or when studying the Word of God. When we enter the House of God we should feel " how fearful is this place! this is nothing but the House of God, and this is the gate of heaven" (Gen. xxviii. 17).

Reverence of God makes us feel ashamed if any frivolity enters our thoughts or passes over our lips, or if we are guilty of any impropriety in our conduct. It makes us cautious with regard to the mentioning of God's name, and keeps us from doing whatever is prohibited in the third commandment. (See p. 6.)

3. *Faith in God's Kindness and Justice.*—We show this faith chiefly in times of trouble. However heavy a trouble may visit us, we must not murmur against God and imagine that we have been wronged by Him. On the contrary, it is our duty to patiently submit to the Will of God. When, therefore, sad news reaches us we say, בָּרוּךְ דַּיָּן אֱמֶת "Blessed be He who is a true Judge," and bear in mind that the All-wise and Omnipotent knows best what we deserve and what is good for us.

4. *Implicit Obedience to His Commands.*—With regard to the Divine commands, we must bear in mind that God is not in want of our service, of our praises and prayers; that it is solely for our good and our true happiness that He made His Will known to us and gave us the opportunity to serve Him and to evidence our love of Him. If we do so, it will give us pleasure to do what He commanded us, however great the sacrifices may be that are demanded of us.

5. *Devotion.*—Part of our time must be devoted to communion with God in prayer, in reflections on Him and His works, in the study of His Will and Word, and in meditating how we can best show ourselves worthy of God's love.

6. *Longing for reconciliation with God*, when we become aware of having acted contrary to His Will. We regret our sins, and with a firm resolve not to repeat them, we return to Him, ask His pardon, and fervently hope that He will grant our petition; for He tells us, "Let him (the sinner) return unto the

E

Lord, and He will have mercy upon him; and to our God, for He will abundantly pardon" (Isa. lv. 7). See p. 20, "Day of Atonement."

B. Duties to our Fellow-creatures.

1. Duties to our Fellow-men.

(a.) General Duties to our Fellow-men.

"*Love thy neighbour as thyself*" (Lev. xix. 18). When once a proselyte came to Hillel, the famous rabbi, with the request to teach him in a few words the principles of Judaism, the rabbi taught him this very precept (T. B. Shabbath 31*a*.) This love is a fundamental principle of Judaism, because it is implied in the doctrine of God's Unity, which it is the mission of Judaism to teach. "Have we not all one Father? has not one God created us? why should we deal treacherously a man against his brother?" (Mal. ii. 10). This principle involves the following rules of conduct:—

(1.) *That which is displeasing to thee, do thou not to thy fellow-men.* We do not like to have our life endangered or our health injured. We must not do anything by which the health of our neighbour might be injured, or his life endangered, or pain and grief be caused to him.

(2.) "*Let the property of thy neighbour be as dear to thee as thy own, and let the honour of thy neighbour be as dear to thee as is thy own*" (Aboth ii. 17, 15). In the same way as we wish our own property to be safe from injury and loss, and our honour from base attack, so is it our duty to protect the property and the honour of our neighbour, and to be most careful lest we cause him injury by any deed or word of ours.

(*a*.) We must not appropriate that which belongs to our neighbour by robbery, theft, or dishonesty, or by assistance and encouragement given to robbers, thieves, or dishonest persons in the pursuance of their unlawful acts. He who buys stolen goods is worse than the thief; the latter only injures the one whom he robs, whilst the former, in addition to this, corrupts the thief, driving him from bad to worse, and makes the way of repentance more difficult for him.

(*b*.) It is base and disgraceful for a man to take advantage of the ignorance or embarrassment of his neighbour for the increase of his own property. Usurers frequently belong to this wicked and disgraceful class of men.

(*c*.) We must not, by falsehood and slander, or by spreading false reports, damage the repute of our neighbour. An "evil tongue" (לְשׁוֹן הָרַע) is a great calamity to society, and separates those who ought to be united in friendship and good-will. It has been said that "calumny kills three,—the slanderer, the one who listens to the slander, and the person slandered."

NOTE.—"Thou shalt not curse the deaf" (Lev. xix. 14), who does not hear what is said, and cannot defend himself. The same is the case with the dead. It is a want of decency and piety to speak ill of the dead, who cannot contradict what is spoken to their discredit or defend themselves.—"Before the blind thou shalt not put a stumbling-block" (*Ibid.*). We must not, in any sense of the word, mislead our fellow-men. When asked by them for advice we must conscientiously counsel what we think best for them.

(d.) It is our duty to protect our neighbour's property and honour. "If thou meetest the ox of thine enemy or his ass going astray, bring it back to him" (Exod. xxiii. 4). If we hear an innocent person slandered, it is our duty to defend him and prove his innocence. Even if we have been wronged by our neighbour, we must not conceive plans of revenge, nor constantly keep the injury in our memory; we must reason with our neighbour and try to convince him of his error or misdeed. "Thou shalt not hate thy brother in thy heart; thou shalt surely reprove thy neighbour, but not bear sin against him. Thou shalt not revenge, and thou shalt not keep a grudge against the children of thy people, but love thy fellow-man like thyself: I am the Lord" (Lev. xix. 17, 18).

Charity, גְּמִילוּת חֶסֶד and צְדָקָה

(e.) There is a more positive form of our love for our fellow-man, and that is charity; in Hebrew it is called צְדָקָה lit. "justice," because the Hebrew considered charity as an act of justice. The general object of charity is to promote, as far as is in our power, the well-being of our fellow-men.

There is one kind of charity which can be extended to rich and poor alike: it is called in Hebrew גְּמִילוּת חֶסֶד "an act of kindness." גְּמִילוּת חֶסֶד includes—

(1.) Visiting the sick (בִּקּוּר חוֹלִים).
(2.) Comforting the mourners (נִחוּם אֲבֵלִים).
(3.) Accompanying the dead to their last resting-place (הֲלְוָיַת הַמֵּת).

(4.) Making peace (הֲבָאַת שָׁלוֹם) between those that are at strife.

(5.) Judging charitably of our neighbours' deeds and words.

A second kind of charity is that practised only towards the poor. It includes—

(1.) Alms-giving (צְדָקָה) for the purpose of temporarily relieving poverty and alleviating suffering.

(2.) Assistance given to the poor towards obtaining a livelihood, by procuring occupation for them, or teaching them a trade.

(3.) Support to the aged and sick, to widows and orphans.

(4.) Helping the poor in the education of their children.

(5.) Comfort and encouragement given by kind words.

(b.) *Special Duties towards our Fellow-men.*

(1.) *Children towards their parents.* " Honour thy father and thy mother" is one of the ten words which God spoke to the Israelites on Mount Sinai.

We honour our parents by considering them as our superiors, as endowed with authority over us, and entitled by reason of their greater experience to be our guides and instructors; by listening respectfully when they speak to us, and by speaking respectfully to them and of them. The love of parents towards their children should find an echo in the hearts of the latter. Parents spare no trouble and shrink from no sacrifice when the well-being of their children demands it. It is the duty of children to show themselves grateful to their parents and to return love for love. We love our parents—

By trying to do everything that pleases them, and to avoid everything that displeases them;

By willing obedience to their commands;

By exerting ourselves to give them pleasure;

By assisting them when, through age, sickness, or misfortune, they are in need of our aid;

By honouring their name and memory after their death; and

By obeying those appointed by them as our guardians in their absence; *e.g.*, an elder brother or sister, a teacher. (Comp. pp. 11–14.)

(2.) Our special duties to other persons may be divided into—

(*a*.) Duties towards our equals.

(*b*.) Duties towards our superiors.

(*c*.) Duties towards our inferiors.

(*a*.) *Duties towards our Equals.*

(1.) Amongst our equals we have some who are closely connected with us by the bond of *friendship*. Special duties towards our friends are, faith in the sincerity of their friendship for us, sincerity and disinterestedness in our friendship for them, readiness to make sacrifices for them, and genuine sympathy for them in their prosperity and in their misfortune.

(2.) *Man and wife* are united by the holy bond of marriage. They owe to each other love, faithfulness, confidence, and untiring endeavour to make each other happy.

(3.) *As citizens* of a state we must take our proper share in all work for the welfare of the state. We must show our loyalty by rendering complete and ungrudging obedience to the laws of our country. When the state is in danger we must evince patriotism, and must not withdraw ourselves from those duties which, under such circumstances, devolve upon every citizen. All our means, our physical and intellectual faculties, must be at the disposal of the country in which we live as citizens.

(4.) *As members of the same religious community*, we must join our brethren in their work for the well-being of the entire body. To separate oneself from the community (פּוֹרֵשׁ עַצְמוֹ מִן הַצִּבּוּר) and to abstain from bearing the common burden has been considered a serious dereliction of duty, and a course of conduct deserving of the strongest condemnation.

(5.) *Towards members of another faith* we have to fulfil all our duties towards our fellow-men as conscientiously as towards members of our own faith. We must show due regard for their religious convictions, and not revile in their presence anything sacred to them. Respect for the religious feelings of others will increase regard for our own religion, and evoke in our neighbours the same respect for our religious feeling.

(6.) Between *employers and employed*, sellers and buyers, strictest honesty must be the basis of all transactions; in cases of dispute a friendly explanation and discussion of the differences will promote the interests of both parties much better than mutual animosity. Each party must bear in mind that its own success depends on the co-operation of the other party and not on its ruin.

(b.) Duties to our Superiors.

To our superiors we owe respect. Such superiors are—

Our *teachers*, who patiently strive to benefit us by their instruction, and whose labours pupils may lighten to their own advantage by due attention and obedience, or aggravate to their own great injury, by inattention and disobedience.

Scholars (תַּלְמִידֵי חֲכָמִים), who, if not directly our teachers, in many ways benefit us by their learning.

The aged (זָקֵן): "Before the hoary head thou shalt rise, and honour the face of the old" (Lev. xix. 32).

The great and good men of our nation, their works and the institutions founded by them: "Do not despise thy mother, though she hath become old" (Prov. xxiii. 22). The feeling of regard in such cases we call *Piety*.

The Magistrates and Judges, who work for the well-being of the citizens.

The Head of the state: "Fear the Lord, O my son, and the king, and do not mix with them that are given to change" (Prov. xxiv. 21).

(c.) Duties to our Inferiors.

We should be kind and charitable to those who are younger than we are, or are less gifted or less fortunate. In our intercourse with them we should show patience, forbearance, and sympathy. Above all, we should try through our words as well as through our example to raise those below us, and improve their physical, intellectual, and moral condition. (See p. 69.)

2. *Kindness to Animals.*

God made man ruler "over the fish of the sea, the birds of the heavens, and all the beasts that move upon the earth." Man has a right to make use of animals for his benefit. They work for him; they serve him as food, provide him with clothing and other necessary things. But though we make use of them, we should treat them with kindness. It is a necessity to make certain beasts work for us, and to kill certain animals for various purposes. But in doing so we must not cause them more pain than is absolutely necessary. (See page 76.) It is a disgraceful act to give pain to animals merely for sport, and to enjoy the sight of their agony. Bull-fights and similar scenes are barbarous, and tend to corrupt and brutalise the heart of man. The more we abstain from cruelty to animals, the more noble and loving is our conduct to our fellow-men likely to be.

The following are instances of kindness to animals enjoined in the Pentateuch :—

"Ye shall not kill an animal and its young on one day" (Lev. xxii. 28).

"If a bird's nest happen to be before thee on the way upon the earth or upon a tree, with young ones or eggs, thou shalt not take the mother with the young. Let the mother go away; then thou mayest take the young ones, in order that it may be well with thee, and thy days be long" (Deut. xxii. 6, 7).

"Thou shalt not muzzle the ox while he is threshing the corn" (*Ibid.* xxv. 4).

C. *Duties to Ourselves.*

Our duties towards God and towards our fellow-men include also most of the duties to ourselves, as the former likewise tend to promote our own well-being.

The principal duty to ourselves is to make the best and worthiest use of that which God in His kindness has given us.

Life and health are gifts which we receive at the hands of Providence; we must consider them as valuable treasures, and must not endanger them without good cause. On the contrary, we must strive, as much as possible, to preserve our life and to improve our health. All pleasures, however agreeable for the moment, must be surrendered if injurious to health.

Man's health is frequently ruined by want of cleanliness, of temperance, of self-control, and of activity.

Cleanliness. It is our duty, whatever our means of livelihood may be, to be most particular with regard to the cleanliness of our body, our clothes, and our dwelling. Experience has taught us that epidemics rage most among those who neglect this duty. To wash the hands before meals is considered by us a religious act.

Temperance is another safeguard of health. From our earliest youth we should train ourselves in the practice of this virtue. We should avoid every kind of excess as the source of evil and misery. A large number of diseases can be traced to indulgence in gratifying the appetites and desires, and especially to excess in eating and drinking. "It is not good to eat much honey" (Prov. xxv. 27).

Self-control is inseparable from temperance. By the acquisition of self-control we are not only enabled to subdue our appetites and desires, but also to prevent the evil consequences of such passions as anger, jealousy, and envy, which undermine our health. If we master our passions, and reflect on their causes, we find in most cases that it was foolish on our part to be angry, jealous, or envious. "Be not hasty in thy spirit to be angry, for anger resteth in the bosom of fools" (Eccles. vii. 9). "Envy is rottenness of the bones" (Prov. xiv. 30).

Activity is a great promoter of health. It has been noticed that persons who have nothing to do are more frequently in ill-health than those who have their regular occupation. Moderate work and exercise make us strong and healthy, while laziness makes us weak and miserable.

Wealth, if acquired in an honest manner, when we have worked hard to gain it, is conducive to our well-being. But in our seeking for wealth we must bear in mind that it is not an end in itself; it serves only as a means for securing our well-being. The struggle for wealth must not suppress the claims of our moral and intellectual life; for if it did so, it would lead to our ruin.

Industry and *honesty* are the two best roads to success and prosperity. "He becometh poor that dealeth with a slack hand: but the hand of the diligent maketh rich" (Prov. x. 4). "Wealth gotten in haste shall be diminished: but he that gathereth by labour shall have increase" (*Ibid.* xiii. 11). Of the virtuous woman it is said, "She looketh well to the ways of her household, and eateth not the bread of idleness" (*Ibid.* xxxi. 27).

Thrift. There are people who by being skilful and industrious earn good wages, and are, nevertheless, frequently in trouble and want. This is, as a rule, the lot of those who are not thrifty; that is, who do not, in good times, save part of their earnings, and keep it for bad times that might come.

The training of our moral and intellectual faculties is of great importance, and must by no means be neglected. We must strive, from our childhood upward, to acquire useful knowledge. Above all, however, we must endeavour to acquire good manners and habits. We must keep our mind pure from evil thoughts, and make it the seat of noble and lofty ideas. Our tongue must be trained in the utterance of that which is true and good. Even in unimportant matters we must weigh our words carefully, so that no untruth may ever come from our lips; under all circumstances our yea must be yea, our nay, nay. "The lip of truth shall be established for ever, but for a moment only the tongue of falsehood" (Prov. xii. 19). In this way we promote our well-being during our life on earth, and secure the Divine blessing for our soul in the world to come.

With regard to the acquisition of good manners and habits we have the general rule: Avoid extremes and observe the golden mean. The following examples may serve as an illustration of this rule: Do not ignore your own self; love yourself and respect yourself, but let not self-love and self-respect grow into selfishness and arrogance. Be temperate and avoid both excess and unnecessary privation. Be neither conceited nor diffident, but self-confident. Be neither obstinate nor weak, but firm. Neither seek nor dread danger, but meet it with courage. Be modest, and guard yourself equally against haughtiness and self-contempt. Do not trust every one, nor suspect every one; but be discreet and cautious. When wronged or insulted, be not indifferent nor passionate, but speak and act calmly and with self-possession; be neither revengeful nor unconcerned, but conciliatory. In spending your earnings show neither niggardliness nor recklessness; be economical. Do not despair, nor be too hopeful, but work, do your duty, and trust in God.

The Dietary Laws.

"Thou shalt not eat any abominable thing" (Deut. xiv. 3). There are certain things which are prohibited by the Law to be used as food; they are called "unclean" (טָמֵא) or "abominable" (תּוֹעֵבָה, שֶׁקֶץ) because the Will of God in forbidding them declared them to be unclean and abominable; by abstaining from them we become holy (קְדוֹשִׁים), and are trained in self-restraint, an essential element in a holy life.

It is also important to remember, though of secondary importance, that the things forbidden in the Law are injurious to man's health. It is a fact that modern science has proved in numerous cases.

A. *Of mineral food* nothing is forbidden except what we know or suspect to be dangerous or injurious.

B. *Of vegetable food* all is permitted that is wholesome, except—

(a.) עָרְלָה. Fruit of a tree during the first three years after its planting (Lev. xix. 23, 24).

(b.) כִּלְאַיִם Divers kinds of grain sown in a vineyard (Deut. xxii. 9).[1]

(c.) חָדָשׁ New grain before the second day of Passover (Lev. xxiii. 14).

---

[1] Similarly the grafting of two different kinds of trees the one upon the other, the cross-breeding of different kinds of cattle, the wearing of garments of linen and wool (שַׁעַטְנֵז) are prohibited (Lev. xix. 19). No reason is given in the Torah for these prohibitions. They are חֻקּוֹת "statutes." They, perhaps, have been intended to teach us the principle of simplicity, and to train us in the virtue of contentment, as a safeguard against undue desire for luxury and superfluity.

C. In reference to animal food we have to observe the following rules:—

1. Care must be taken that the killing of animals and the consuming of their flesh shall not tend to create savage and cruel habits. It is therefore forbidden—

(*a.*) To cut off a piece of flesh of a living animal for our food (אֵבֶר מִן הַחַי "limb of a living animal").

(*b.*) To kill the parent with its young on the same day (Lev. xxii. 28; comp. Deut. xxii. 6).

(*c.*) To give unnecessary pain to the animal in killing it. On this principle the regulations for killing animals (שְׁחִיטָה) are based.

(*d.*) To eat the blood of beasts and birds (Lev. xvii. 12, 14). The blood contained in the meat is removed as far as possible by having the meat soaked in water for half an hour, and then kept covered with salt for an hour, the salt being again removed by rinsing. This process is called *kasher*; that is, preparing the meat so as to make it כָּשֵׁר "fit for food."

2. The flesh of an animal that has died of itself (נְבֵלָה) is forbidden as injurious to health. The flesh of animals properly killed, but found on examination to have been affected with some dangerous disease, is forbidden, and called טְרֵפָה.[1]

3. With regard to the distinction between animals allowed for food and those forbidden, the animals are divided into: בְּהֵמָה "cattle," חַיָּה "beast," עוֹף "bird," and שֶׁרֶץ "creeping thing."

---

[1] טְרֵפָה originally designated meat of animals torn by wild beasts, but it is now used to describe meat forbidden by the Law. All permitted food is *kasher* (כָּשֵׁר).

(*a.*) With regard to cattle and beasts, the rule is given, "Whatsoever parteth the hoof and is cloven-footed and cheweth the cud, that you may eat" (Lev. xi. 3).[1]

(*b.*) A number of birds are enumerated as forbidden (*Ibid.* xi. 13 *seq.*), but being uncertain as to the exact meaning of the names of many of the birds, we only use for food such birds as are traditionally known as "clean" birds.

(*c.*) Fish with scales and fins are permitted; others are "unclean" (*Ibid.* xi. 9 *seq.*).

4. Those portions of the fat of cattle which used to be burnt upon the altar as part of the sacrifices are forbidden. These are called חֵלֶב "forbidden fat."

5. The "sinew that shrank," גִּיד הַנָּשֶׁה (Gen. xxxii. 33).

NOTE.—This law shall remind us of the wrestling of Jacob with the man who attacked him, which forms a type of Israel's fight against the evil threatening him from within and from without, and teach us the lesson that, despite temporary troubles and struggles, Israel will ultimately be victorious.

6. "Thou shalt not seethe the kid in its mother's milk" (Exod. xxiii. 19). This law is explained by Tradition as forbidding all mixture of meat and milk (בָּשָׂר בְּחָלָב).

NOTE.—The literal meaning of the verse points to the duty of self-restraint, that we must not fall with greediness upon the first-ripe fruit, or upon the young immediately after their birth.

---

[1] The milk of forbidden cattle and beasts and the eggs of forbidden birds are likewise forbidden.

TRADITION.

(FOR STANDARD VI.)

THE words, "And thou shalt kill (the animal) *as I have commanded thee*" (Deut. xii. 21), imply that the manner of killing had been commanded; and as this subject is not further referred to in the written Law, it follows that there must have existed another unwritten or oral Law that contained details and explanations of the commandments of the written Law. Furthermore, the man who gathered sticks on Sabbath was put to death; the Israelites must have learnt from Moses that the prohibition of work implied the prohibition of gathering sticks (Num. xv. 32 *seq.*). Such explanations and details were at first handed down from generation to generation by word of mouth. "Moses received the Law from Sinai (that is, from Him who had revealed Himself on Sinai), and handed it down to Joshua, and Joshua to the Elders, the Elders to the Prophets, and the Prophets to the men of the Great Synagogue" in the days of Ezra the Scribe (Aboth i. 1). It was then further transmitted from generation to generation till the time of *Rabbi Jehuda hannasi*, called the Holy, who collected and sifted the traditions, and arranged them, according to their contents, in a code, called *Mishnah* (Oral Law). The Mishnah consists of six sections (שִׁשָׁה סְדָרִים "Orders)," viz., I. זְרָעִים On Divine worship and laws concerning seeds. II. מוֹעֵד On Sabbath and Festivals. III. נָשִׁים On marriage. IV. נְזִיקִין (lit. damages), Civil and criminal laws. V. קָדָשִׁים On sacrifices. VI. טַהֲרוֹת (lit. purities), On things clean and unclean.

When these had been written down, their contents formed the subject of comment, criticism, explanation, and discussion in the Academies. These were collected, and are called the *Gemara*, גְּמָרָא. Mishnah and Gemara together are called Talmud. We have the Talmud in two different forms; the one was written in the Babylonian schools, and is called the *Babylonian Talmud* (תַּלְמוּד בַּבְלִי); the other in Palestine, and is called the *Palestine or Jerusalem Talmud* (תַּלְמוּד יְרוּשַׁלְמִי).

The laws contained in the Talmud are intermingled with a mass of other material, such as meditations, narratives, legends, exhortations, and parables. To make them more easily available, they have been collected, and systematically arranged in two great works: (1) Mishneh Torah, or *Yad hachazakah*, by Rabbi Moses Maimonides, in fourteen books; and (2) *Shulchan Aruch*, by Rabbi Joseph Karo, in four parts—

    I. Divine worship, Sabbath, and Festivals (אֹרַח חַיִּים).

    II. Laws regulating Jewish household and home life (יוֹרֶה דֵעָה).

    III. Marriage Laws (אֶבֶן הָעֵזֶר).

    IV. Civil Laws (חֹשֶׁן מִשְׁפָּט).

The traditional laws contained in these works may be divided as follows:—

    (1.) Laws not directly *contained in* the Pentateuch,

but *derived from* the text of the Law, by certain rules of interpretation (מִן הַתּוֹרָה).

(2.) Laws not connected with the text of the Law, but traced back to the time of Moses, הֲלָכָה לְמֹשֶׁה מִסִּינַי

(3.) Regulations for the prevention of breaking the Law; they are called a fence for the Torah, גְזֵרוֹת

(4.) Laws and regulations laid down from time to time as circumstances demanded, תְּקָנוֹת

(5.) Practices not commanded by any authority, but hallowed by age and generally accepted as laws, מִנְהָגִים

NOTE.—We owe obedience to the laws which emanated from the chief religious authority of the nation after Moses. For we are commanded, "According to the tenor of the law which they —the priests, the Levites, and the judge—shall teach thee, and according to the judgment which they shall tell thee, thou shalt do: thou shalt not turn aside from the word which they shall tell thee, to the right hand, nor to the left" (Deut. xvii. 11).

THE JEWISH CALENDAR.

The Jews have adopted the Era of the Creation, and count at present 5650. The ordinary year consists of 12, the leap-year of 13 months. As the months are determined by the revolution of the moon round the earth, and the moon completes her circuit in about $29\frac{1}{2}$ days, 2 months have together about 59 days. Therefore the Hebrew months have alternately 29 and 30 days.

The 1st day of the month and the 30th are called New-moon (רֹאשׁ חֹדֶשׁ). We have therefore alternately one and two days רֹאשׁ חֹדֶשׁ; only Kislev and Tebeth are irregular. Nisan has 30 days, Iyar 29, Sivan 30, Tammuz 29, Ab 30, Ellul 29, Tishri 30, Heshvan 29 or 30, Kislev 29 or 30, Tebeth 29, Shebat 30, Adar

29 (in a leap-year Adar 30, and Adar-sheni 29). Accordingly *Rosh-chodesh* of Nisan, Sivan, Ab, Tishri, Shebat, is one day; of Iyar, Tammuz, Ellul, Cheshvan, Adar (and in a leap-year Adar-sheni) 2 days; Kislev and Tebeth respectively 1 and 2, or both 1 or both 2 days Rosh-chodesh. The Hebrew year, consisting of 12 lunar months, is shorter than the solar year by 11 (or 10 or 12) days. In 3 years the difference would amount to more than a month, and Nisan would thus fall in winter instead of spring. But as Passover is commanded to be kept in the month Abib ("the ears of corn"), *i.e.*, in the spring, a month must be added every 2 or 3 years; and such a year of 13 months is called a leap-year. Each cycle of 19 years has 7 leap-years, viz., the 3rd, 6th, 8th, 11th, 14th, 17th, and 19th.

APPENDIX.

I.

1. *Nisan.*—The Sabbath before Passover is called שַׁבָּת הַגָּדוֹל "the Great Sabbath," on account of the importance of the approaching festival.

    14th: עֶרֶב פֶּסַח "the Eve of Passover." Fast of the First-born.

    15th to 22nd: פֶּסַח "Passover."

    16th: "Beginning of counting the Omer," סְפִירַת הָעוֹמֶר

    17th to 20th: חוֹל הַמּוֹעֵד "Half-holydays."

    23rd: אִסְרוּ חַג "Farewell to the Festival."

2. *Iyar.*—14th: פֶּסַח שֵׁנִי "Second Passover" (Num. xi. 9 *sqq.*).

    18th ל״ג בָּעוֹמֶר the 33rd of the Omer. "Scholar's feast."

    שֵׁנִי חֲמִישִׁי וְשֵׁנִי Fasts kept by some, on the first Monday, Thursday, and Monday succeeding each other in the month, in order to atone for sins they may have committed on the Holydays.

3. *Sivan.*—3rd, 4th, and 5th: שְׁלֹשֶׁת יְמֵי הַגְבָּלָה "The three days of bordering" (Exod. xix. 10–12).

    5th: עֶרֶב שָׁבוּעוֹת "The eve of the Feast of Weeks."

    6th and 7th: שָׁבוּעוֹת "Feast of Weeks," also called "Pentecost."

    8th: אִסְרוּ חַג "Farewell to the Festival."

4. *Tammuz.*—17th: "Fast of Tammuz," שִׁבְעָה עָשָׂר בְּתַמּוּז
5. *Ab.*—"Sabbath before the Fast," שַׁבַּת חָזוֹן (see p. 33).
9th: "Fast of Ab," תִּשְׁעָה בְּאָב
"Sabbath after the Fast," שַׁבַּת נַחֲמוּ (*ibid.*)
15th: חֲמִשָּׁה עָשָׂר בְּאָב "15th of Ab." Reconciliation of the Benjamites with the other Israelites (Judges xxi.)
6. *Ellul.*—יְמֵי הַסְּלִיחוֹת "Days of propitiatory prayers," beginning on the first day of the month according to the Spanish Rite, and according to the German Rite, on the Sunday before רֹאשׁ הַשָּׁנָה
29th: עֶרֶב רֹאשׁ הַשָּׁנָה "The eve of New-year."
7. *Tishri.*—1st and 2nd: "New-year," רֹאשׁ הַשָּׁנָה
3rd: "Fast of Gedaliah," צוֹם גְּדַלְיָהוּ
1st to 10th: "The ten penitential days," עֲשֶׂרֶת יְמֵי תְשׁוּבָה
"The Sabbath after New-year," שַׁבָּת שׁוּבָה (see p. 22).
9th: עֶרֶב יוֹם כִּפּוּר "The eve of the Day of Atonement."
10th: יוֹם הַכִּפּוּרִים or יוֹם כִּפּוּר "The Day of Atonement."
14th: עֶרֶב סֻכּוֹת "The eve of Sukkoth."
15th to 21st: סֻכּוֹת "Feast of Tabernacles."
17th to 21st: חוֹל הַמּוֹעֵד "Half-holyday."
21st: הוֹשַׁעְנָא רַבָּא "The Great Hoshana Service."
22nd and 23rd: שְׁמִינִי עֲצֶרֶת "Feast of the eighth day."
23rd: שִׂמְחַת תּוֹרָה "Rejoicing of the Law."
24th: אִסְרוּ חַג "Farewell to the Festival."
8. *Heshvan.*—שֵׁנִי חֲמִישִׁי וְשֵׁנִי "The Fast of 'Monday, Thursday, and Monday,' kept by some at the end of the month."
9. *Kislev.*—25th to 2nd (or 3rd) of *Tebeth:* חֲנֻכָּה "Feast of Dedication."
10. *Tebeth.*—10th: עֲשָׂרָה בְּטֵבֵת "The Fast of Tebeth."

11. *Shebat.*—15th : חֲמִשָׁה עָשָׂר בִּשְׁבָט "New-year for trees."
The last Sabbath in the month (or the first in Adar), שַׁבָּת שְׁקָלִים " The Sabbath of Shekalim." Exod. xxx. 11–16 is read in addition to the weekly portion.

12. *Adar.*—7th : Anniversary of death of Moses.
Sabbath before Purim, שַׁבָּת זָכוֹר (Deut. xxv. 17–19).
13th : תַּעֲנִית אֶסְתֵּר "Fast of Esther."
14th : Purim, פּוּרִים "The Feast of Lots."
15th : שׁוּשַׁן פּוּרִים "Purim of Shushan."
The last Sabbath but one, שַׁבָּת פָּרָה Num. xix. is read as an extra lesson.
The last Sabbath in the month, or the first in Nisan, if New-moon, שַׁבָּת הַחוֹדֶשׁ Exod. xii. 1–20 is read as an extra lesson.

[13. *Adar Sheni.*—פּוּרִים, תַּעֲנִית אֶסְתֵּר, שַׁבָּת זָכוֹר, שׁוּשַׁן פּוּרִים, שַׁבָּת פָּרָה, and שַׁבָּת הַחֹדֶשׁ which in an ordinary year are observed in Adar, are in a leap-year kept in Adar Sheni; and שַׁבָּת שְׁקָלִים either on the last Sabbath in Adar, or on the first day of Adar Sheni.]

APPENDIX II.

THE BOOKS OF THE BIBLE, תנ״ך (= תּוֹרָה, נְבִיאִים, כְּתוּבִים).

I. תּוֹרָה *Law*, also called חוּמָשׁ *Pentateuch* (Five books). It contains besides the Law the history from Adam to the death of Moses. It is divided into five books (סְפָרִים), each of which is subdivided into weekly portions (סְדְרָא), and these again into seven portions, of which each is called פָּרָשָׁה. The following are the five books:—

1. בְּרֵאשִׁית *Genesis*: contains the history of the Creation, of Adam and his sons, of Noah and the flood, and of the Patriarchs to the death of Joseph.
2. שְׁמוֹת *Exodus*: contains the history of the Israelites in Egypt, their departure from Egypt, the Revelation on Mount Sinai, and the construction of the Tabernacle.
3. וַיִּקְרָא *Leviticus*.—Laws concerning sacrifices; dietary and sanitary laws, the sanctification of man.
4. בַּמִּדְבָּר *Numbers*.—History of the Israelites during their journeys in the wilderness from Sinai to the borders of Moab.
5. דְּבָרִים *Deuteronomy*.—Moses addresses the people, and exhorts them to be faithful to God and His Law.

II. נְבִיאִים *Prophets*.
   A. נְבִיאִים רִאשׁוֹנִים *Earlier Prophets*: containing the history of the Israelites from the conquest of Pales-

tine by Joshua to the destruction of the Temple of
Jerusalem by Nebuchadnezzar, king of Babylon.

(a.) יְהוֹשֻׁעַ *Joshua.*—The conquest and division of the Holy
Land.

(b.) שֹׁפְטִים *Judges.*—The period of the Judges between
the death of Joshua and the birth of Samuel.

(c.) שְׁמוּאֵל א׳ ב׳ *Two Books of Samuel.*—The history of
Samuel and Saul, the earlier history of David (first
book), and the reign of David (second book).

(d.) מְלָכִים א׳ ב׳ *Two Books of Kings.*—Death of David,
reign of Solomon, division of the realm into the
kingdoms of Judah and Israel, kings of Judah to
Joshaphat, and of Israel to Ahab (first book), the
successors of Ahab to the occupation of the country
by the Assyrians, and the successors of Joshaphat
to the beginning of the Babylonian exile (2nd book).

B. נְבִיאִים אַחֲרוֹנִים *Latter Prophets:* contain exhortations
to faith in God and obedience to His command-
ments, addresses of rebuke, and words of comfort.

1. יְשַׁעְיָהוּ *Isaiah.*—During the reigns of Uzziah, Jotham,
Ahaz, and Hezekiah.

2. יִרְמְיָה *Jeremiah.*—From the reign of Josiah to the
Babylonian exile.

3. יְחֶזְקֵאל *Ezekiel.*—During the Babylonian exile.

4. תְּרֵי עָשָׂר (The twelve) *Minor Prophets.*

הוֹשֵׁעַ Hosea.	
יוֹאֵל Joel.	
עָמוֹס Amos.	Contemporaries of Isaiah.
עוֹבַדְיָה Obadiah.	
יוֹנָה Jonah.	
מִיכָה Micah.	

נַחוּם Nahum. ⎫
חֲבַקּוּק Habakkuk. ⎬ From the end of the Assyrian invasion to the beginning of the Babylonian invasion.
צְפַנְיָה Zephaniah. ⎭

חַגַּי Haggai. ⎫
זְכַרְיָה Zechariah. ⎬ After the return of the Jews from the Babylonian exile.
מַלְאָכִי Malachi. ⎭

III. כְּתוּבִים *Holy Writings or Hagiographa.*
  1. תְּהִלִּים (lit. Praises), Psalms of David and several other writers.
  2. מִשְׁלֵי *Proverbs of Solomon.*
  3. אִיּוֹב *Job:* contains the history of a pious man who suffered exceedingly, yet remained faithful to God, and the discussions of Job and his friends on the goodness and justice of God.
  4. שִׁיר הַשִּׁירִים *Song of Solomon.*—Songs in which the relation between God and Israel is supposed to be figuratively represented as that between Bridegroom and Bride.
  5. רוּת *Ruth.*—The history of Ruth, her kindness and faithfulness to her husband and his kinsfolk.
  6. אֵיכָה *Lamentations.*—Lamentations of Jeremiah for the destruction of the Temple in Jerusalem by Nebucadnezzar, and the exile of the Israelites.
  7. קֹהֶלֶת *Ecclesiastes.*— Reflections on the vanity of human life.
  8. אֶסְתֵּר *Esther.*—The history of Haman's plot against the Jews, and its defeat through Mordecai and Esther.

  These five books are called "the five rolls," חָמֵשׁ מְגִלּוֹת and are read on Passover, Festival of Weeks, 9th of Ab, Festival of Tabernacles, and Purim respectively.

APPENDIX. 91

9. דָּנִיֵאל *Daniel.*—The history and visions of Daniel during the Babylonian exile.
10. עֶזְרָא *Ezra.*—The history of the return of the Jews from the Babylonian exile, and the rebuilding of the Temple.
11. נְחֶמְיָה *Nehemiah.*—The rebuilding of the walls of Jerusalem.
12. דִּבְרֵי הַיָּמִים א׳ וב׳ *The two Books of Chronicles.*—Genealogies of the tribes of Israel, and the history of the kingdom of Judah.

APOCRYPHA.

When the Canon of the Holy Scriptures was fixed, there were many other instructive and edifying books written by Jewish authors, but they were not considered inspired writings, and were therefore not included among the Holy Scriptures. They are called Apocrypha, "hidden" or "laid aside;" that is, not added to the Holy Scriptures. The principal books of the Apocrypha are the following:—

1. Two books of proverbs and maxims:
   The Wisdom of Solomon.
   Ecclesiasticus.
2. Additions to Biblical books:
   The Book of Baruch, additions to Jeremiah.
   Additions to the Book of Daniel.
   Additions to Ezra.
3. Narratives:
   The Books of the Maccabees.
   The Book of Judith.
   The Book of Tobit.

APPENDIX III.

The Ten Commandments עֲשֶׂרֶת הַדִּבְּרוֹת

וַיְדַבֵּר אֱלֹהִים אֵת כָּל־ הַדְּבָרִים הָאֵלֶּה לֵאמֹר:

א—אָנֹכִי יְיָ אֱלֹהֶיךָ אֲשֶׁר הוֹצֵאתִיךָ מֵאֶרֶץ מִצְרַיִם מִבֵּית עֲבָדִים:

ב—לֹא־יִהְיֶה לְךָ אֱלֹהִים אֲחֵרִים עַל־פָּנָי: לֹא תַעֲשֶׂה לְךָ פֶסֶל וְכָל־תְּמוּנָה אֲשֶׁר בַּשָּׁמַיִם מִמַּעַל וַאֲשֶׁר בָּאָרֶץ מִתַּחַת וַאֲשֶׁר בַּמַּיִם מִתַּחַת לָאָרֶץ: לֹא תִשְׁתַּחֲוֶה לָהֶם וְלֹא תָעָבְדֵם כִּי אָנֹכִי יְיָ אֱלֹהֶיךָ אֵל קַנָּא פֹּקֵד עֲוֹן אָבֹת עַל בָּנִים עַל־שִׁלֵּשִׁים וְעַל־רִבֵּעִים לְשֹׂנְאָי: וְעֹשֶׂה חֶסֶד לַאֲלָפִים לְאֹהֲבַי וּלְשֹׁמְרֵי מִצְוֹתָי:

ג—לֹא־תִשָּׂא אֶת־שֵׁם־יְיָ־אֱלֹהֶיךָ לַשָּׁוְא כִּי לֹא יְנַקֶּה יְיָ אֵת אֲשֶׁר־יִשָּׂא אֶת־שְׁמוֹ לַשָּׁוְא:

ד—זָכוֹר אֶת־יוֹם הַשַּׁבָּת לְקַדְּשׁוֹ: שֵׁשֶׁת יָמִים תַּעֲבֹד וְעָשִׂיתָ כָּל־מְלַאכְתֶּךָ: וְיוֹם הַשְּׁבִיעִי שַׁבָּת לַיְיָ אֱלֹהֶיךָ לֹא תַעֲשֶׂה כָל־מְלָאכָה אַתָּה וּבִנְךָ וּבִתֶּךָ עַבְדְּךָ וַאֲמָתְךָ וּבְהֶמְתֶּךָ וְגֵרְךָ אֲשֶׁר בִּשְׁעָרֶיךָ: כִּי שֵׁשֶׁת־יָמִים עָשָׂה יְיָ אֶת־הַשָּׁמַיִם וְאֶת־הָאָרֶץ אֶת־הַיָּם וְאֶת־כָּל־אֲשֶׁר בָּם וַיָּנַח בַּיּוֹם הַשְּׁבִיעִי עַל־כֵּן בֵּרַךְ יְיָ אֶת־יוֹם הַשַּׁבָּת וַיְקַדְּשֵׁהוּ:

ה—כַּבֵּד אֶת־אָבִיךָ וְאֶת־אִמֶּךָ לְמַעַן יַאֲרִכוּן יָמֶיךָ עַל הָאֲדָמָה אֲשֶׁר־יְיָ אֱלֹהֶיךָ נֹתֵן לָךְ:

ו—לֹא תִּרְצָח:

ז—לֹא תִּנְאָף:

ח—לֹא תִּגְנֹב:

ט—לֹא תַעֲנֶה בְרֵעֲךָ עֵד שָׁקֶר:

י—לֹא תַחְמֹד בֵּית רֵעֶךָ: לֹא תַחְמֹד אֵשֶׁת רֵעֶךָ וְעַבְדּוֹ וַאֲמָתוֹ וְשׁוֹרוֹ וַחֲמֹרוֹ וְכֹל אֲשֶׁר לְרֵעֶךָ:

APPENDIX IV.

The Thirteen Creeds שְׁלֹשׁ עֶשְׂרֵה עִקָּרִים
אֲנִי מַאֲמִין בֶּאֱמוּנָה שְׁלֵמָה

א—שֶׁהַבּוֹרֵא יִתְבָּרַךְ שְׁמוֹ הוּא בּוֹרֵא וּמַנְהִיג לְכָל הַבְּרוּאִים וְהוּא לְבַדּוֹ עָשָׂה וְעוֹשֶׂה וְיַעֲשֶׂה לְכָל הַמַּעֲשִׂים:

ב—שֶׁהַבּוֹרֵא יִתְבָּרַךְ שְׁמוֹ הוּא יָחִיד וְאֵין יְחִידוּת כָּמוֹהוּ בְּשׁוּם פָּנִים וְהוּא לְבַדּוֹ אֱלֹהֵינוּ הָיָה הֹוֶה וְיִהְיֶה:

ג—שֶׁהַבּוֹרֵא יִתְבָּרַךְ שְׁמוֹ אֵינוֹ גוּף וְלֹא יַשִּׂיגוּהוּ מַשִּׂיגֵי הַגּוּף וְאֵין לוֹ שׁוּם דִּמְיוֹן כְּלָל:

ד—שֶׁהַבּוֹרֵא יִתְבָּרַךְ שְׁמוֹ הוּא רִאשׁוֹן וְהוּא אַחֲרוֹן:

ה—שֶׁהַבּוֹרֵא יִתְבָּרַךְ שְׁמוֹ לוֹ לְבַדּוֹ רָאוּי לְהִתְפַּלֵּל וְאֵין רָאוּי לְהִתְפַּלֵּל לְזוּלָתוֹ:

ו—שֶׁכָּל דִּבְרֵי הַנְּבִיאִים אֱמֶת:

ז—שֶׁנְּבוּאַת מֹשֶׁה רַבֵּנוּ עָלָיו הַשָּׁלוֹם הָיְתָה אֲמִתִּית וְשֶׁהוּא הָיָה אָב לַנְּבִיאִים לַקּוֹדְמִים לְפָנָיו וְלַבָּאִים אַחֲרָיו:

ח—שֶׁכָּל הַתּוֹרָה הַמְּצוּיָה עַתָּה בְּיָדֵינוּ הִיא הַנְּתוּנָה לְמֹשֶׁה רַבֵּנוּ עָלָיו הַשָּׁלוֹם:

ט—שֶׁזֹּאת הַתּוֹרָה לֹא תְהִי מֻחְלֶפֶת וְלֹא תְהִי תּוֹרָה אַחֶרֶת מֵאֵת הַבּוֹרֵא יִתְבָּרַךְ שְׁמוֹ:

י—שֶׁהַבּוֹרֵא יִתְבָּרַךְ שְׁמוֹ יוֹדֵעַ כָּל מַעֲשֵׂי בְנֵי אָדָם וְכָל מַחְשְׁבוֹתָם שֶׁנֶּאֱמַר הַיֹּצֵר יַחַד לִבָּם הַמֵּבִין אֶל כָּל מַעֲשֵׂיהֶם:

יא—שֶׁהַבּוֹרֵא יִתְבָּרַךְ שְׁמוֹ גּוֹמֵל טוֹב לְשׁוֹמְרֵי מִצְוֹתָיו וּמַעֲנִישׁ לְעוֹבְרֵי מִצְוֹתָיו:

יב—בְּבִיאַת הַמָּשִׁיחַ וְאַף עַל פִּי שֶׁיִּתְמַהְמֵהַּ עִם כָּל זֶה אֲחַכֶּה-לּוֹ בְּכָל יוֹם שֶׁיָּבוֹא:

יג—שֶׁתִּהְיֶה תְּחִיַּת הַמֵּתִים בְּעֵת שֶׁתַּעֲלֶה רָצוֹן מֵאֵת הַבּוֹרֵא יִתְבָּרַךְ שְׁמוֹ וְיִתְעַלֶּה זִכְרוֹ לָעַד וּלְנֵצַח נְצָחִים:

APPENDIX V.

Texts of Moral Duties.

וְאָהַבְתָּ אֵת יְיָ אֱלֹהֶיךָ בְּכָל לְבָבְךָ וּבְכָל נַפְשְׁךָ וּבְכָל מְאֹדֶךָ:
(Deut. vi. 5.)

וְאָהַבְתָּ לְרֵעֲךָ כָּמוֹךָ אֲנִי יְיָ: (Lev. xix. 18.)

לֹא־תִשְׂנָא אֶת־אָחִיךָ בִּלְבָבֶךָ הוֹכֵחַ תּוֹכִיחַ אֶת־עֲמִיתֶךָ וְלֹא־תִשָּׂא עָלָיו חֵטְא: (Ibid. 17.)

לֹא־תִקֹּם וְלֹא־תִטֹּר אֶת־בְּנֵי עַמֶּךָ: (Ibid. 18.)

וְגֵר לֹא תִלְחָץ וְאַתֶּם יְדַעְתֶּם אֶת־נֶפֶשׁ הַגֵּר כִּי־גֵרִים הֱיִיתֶם בְּאֶרֶץ מִצְרָיִם: (Ex. xxiii. 9.)

וְכִי־יָגוּר אִתְּךָ גֵּר בְּאַרְצְכֶם לֹא תוֹנוּ אֹתוֹ: כְּאֶזְרָח מִכֶּם יִהְיֶה לָכֶם הַגֵּר הַגָּר אִתְּכֶם וְאָהַבְתָּ לוֹ כָּמוֹךָ אֲנִי יְיָ אֱלֹהֵיכֶם: (Lev. xix. 34.)

כָּל אַלְמָנָה וְיָתוֹם לֹא תְעַנּוּן: (Ex. xx. 22.)

לֹא־תַעֲשֹׁק שָׂכִיר עָנִי וְאֶבְיוֹן מֵאַחֶיךָ אוֹ מִגֵּרְךָ אֲשֶׁר בְּאַרְצְךָ בִּשְׁעָרֶיךָ: (Deut. xxiv. 14.)

פָּתֹחַ תִּפְתַּח אֶת־יָדְךָ לְאָחִיךָ לַעֲנִיֶּךָ וּלְאֶבְיֹנְךָ בְּאַרְצֶךָ: (Ibid. xv. 11.)

אִם־כֶּסֶף תַּלְוֶה אֶת־עַמִּי אֶת־הֶעָנִי עִמָּךְ לֹא־תִהְיֶה לוֹ כְּנֹשֶׁה לֹא־תְשִׂימוּן עָלָיו נֶשֶׁךְ: (Exod. xxii. 25.)

מִפְּנֵי שֵׂיבָה תָּקוּם וְהָדַרְתָּ פְּנֵי זָקֵן וְיָרֵאתָ מֵאֱלֹהֶיךָ אֲנִי יְיָ:
(Lev. xix. 32.)

קְדֹשִׁים תִּהְיוּ כִּי קָדוֹשׁ אֲנִי יְיָ אֱלֹהֵיכֶם: (Ibid. 2.)

לֹא תִּגְנֹבוּ וְלֹא־תְכַחֲשׁוּ וְלֹא־תְשַׁקְּרוּ אִישׁ בַּעֲמִיתוֹ: (Ibid. 11.)

לֹא־תַעֲשׂוּ עָוֶל בַּמִּשְׁפָּט בַּמִּדָּה בַּמִּשְׁקָל וּבַמְּשׂוּרָה: (Ibid. 35.)

וְכִי־תִמְכְּרוּ מִמְכָּר לַעֲמִיתֶךָ אוֹ קָנֹה מִיַּד עֲמִיתֶךָ אַל־תּוֹנוּ אִישׁ אֶת־אָחִיו:
(Ibid. xxv. 14.)

לֹא־תֵלֵךְ רָכִיל בְּעַמֶּךָ: (Lev. xix. 16.)
נְצֹר לְשׁוֹנְךָ מֵרָע וּשְׂפָתֶיךָ מִדַּבֵּר מִרְמָה:
רַחֲצוּ הִזַּכּוּ הָסִירוּ רֹעַ מַעַלְלֵיכֶם מִנֶּגֶד עֵינָי חִדְלוּ הָרֵעַ: לִמְדוּ הֵיטֵב: (Isa. i. 16, 17.)
הִגִּיד לְךָ אָדָם מַה־טּוֹב וּמַה יְיָ דּוֹרֵשׁ מִמְּךָ כִּי אִם עֲשׂוֹת מִשְׁפָּט וְאַהֲבַת חֶסֶד וְהַצְנֵעַ לֶכֶת עִם אֱלֹהֶיךָ: (Mic. vi. 6.)

APPENDIX VI.

BENEDICTIONS בְּרָכוֹת

The first part of a בְּרָכָה is invariably בָּרוּךְ אַתָּה יְיָ אֱלֹהֵינוּ מֶלֶךְ הָעוֹלָם "Blessed art thou, O Lord our God, King of the Universe."

The second part varies according to the occasion for the בְּרָכָה ; viz. :—

Before partaking of bread, הַמּוֹצִיא לֶחֶם מִן הָאָרֶץ "who hast brought forth bread out of the earth."

Before partaking of cake, בּוֹרֵא מִינֵי מְזוֹנוֹת "who hast created various kinds of food."

Before partaking of wine, בּוֹרֵא פְּרִי הַגֶּפֶן "who hast created the fruit of the vine."

Before partaking of fruit that grows on trees and shrubs, בּוֹרֵא פְּרִי הָעֵץ "who hast created the fruit of the tree."

Before partaking of other fruit, בּוֹרֵא פְּרִי הָאֲדָמָה "who hast created the fruit of the earth."

Before partaking of anything not included in the above objects, שֶׁהַכֹּל נִהְיָה בִּדְבָרוֹ "by whose word everything has come into existence."

On enjoying a pleasant fragrance, בּוֹרֵא מִינֵי בְשָׂמִים "who hast created various kinds of spices."

On hearing a thunderstorm, שֶׁכֹּחוֹ וּגְבוּרָתוֹ מָלֵא עוֹלָם "whose strength and power filleth the Universe."

On seeing lightning, עֹשֶׂה מַעֲשֵׂה בְרֵאשִׁית "who repeatest the act of Creation."

APPENDIX.

On seeing the sea, שֶׁעָשָׂה אֶת־הַיָּם הַגָּדוֹל "who hast made the great sea."

On seeing a rainbow, זוֹכֵר הַבְּרִית וְנֶאֱמָן בִּבְרִיתוֹ וְקַיָּם בְּמַאֲמָרוֹ "who rememberest the covenant, art faithful to Thy covenant, and keepest Thy promise."

On seeing in Nisan the first blossoming trees, שֶׁלֹּא חִסַּר בְּעוֹלָמוֹ דָּבָר וּבָרָא בוֹ בְּרִיּוֹת טוֹבוֹת וְאִילָנוֹת טוֹבִים לְהַנּוֹת בָּהֶם בְּנֵי אָדָם "who hast not omitted anything in the world made by Thee, and hast created in it goodly creatures and goodly trees wherewith to benefit the children of man."

On tasting new fruit, putting on new garments, or entering a new house, שֶׁהֶחֱיָנוּ וְקִיְּמָנוּ וְהִגִּיעָנוּ לַזְּמַן הַזֶּה "who hast given us life, preserved us, and permitted us to reach this season."

On hearing good news, הַטּוֹב וְהַמֵּטִיב "who art good, and causest others to be good."

On hearing sad news, דַּיַּן אֱמֶת "true Judge."

After having partaken of any food or drink, except bread, cake, wine, figs, dates, and pomegranates, בּוֹרֵא נְפָשׁוֹת רַבּוֹת וְחֶסְרוֹנָן עַל כָּל מַה־שֶּׁבָּרָא לְהַחֲיוֹת בָּהֶם נֶפֶשׁ כָּל חַי בָּרוּךְ חַי הָעוֹלָמִים "who hast created many living beings and the supply of their different wants, in addition to all that thou hast created for the maintenance of all living; blessed art Thou that livest for ever."

A בְּרָכָה before the performance of a religious duty begins thus: בָּרוּךְ אַתָּה יְיָ אֱלֹהֵינוּ מֶלֶךְ הָעוֹלָם אֲשֶׁר קִדְּשָׁנוּ בְּמִצְוֹתָיו וְצִוָּנוּ "blessed art thou, O Lord, our God, King of the Universe, who hast sanctified us by Thy commandments, and commanded us."

The reference to the special religious duty forms the second part of the בְּרָכָה

Before washing the hands, עַל נְטִילַת יָדַיִם "for washing the hands."

G

Before putting on the *arba kanfoth*,[1] עַל מִצְוַת צִיצִת "concerning the commandment of *tsitsith*."

Before putting on the *talith*,[1] לְהִתְעַטֵּף בַּצִּיצִת "to wrap ourselves in a garment with *tsitsith*."

Before putting on the *tefillin*,[1] לְהָנִיחַ תְּפִלִּין "to lay *tefillin*," and עַל מִצְוַת תְּפִלִּין "concerning the commandment of *tefillin*."

Before taking the *lulabh*, עַל נְטִילַת לוּלָב "concerning the taking of the *lulabh*."

Before kindling the Sabbath lights, לְהַדְלִיק נֵר שֶׁל שַׁבָּת "to kindle the Sabbath lights."

Before kindling the Festival lights, לְהַדְלִיק נֵר שֶׁל יוֹם טוֹב "to kindle the Festival lights;" or, לְהַדְלִיק נֵר שַׁבָּת וְיוֹם טוֹב if the Festival happens to be on Sabbath.

Before kindling lights on the eve of the Day of Atonement לְהַדְלִיק נֵר שֶׁל יוֹם הַכִּפּוּרִים "to kindle the lights for the Day of Atonement."

Before fixing the *mezuzah*, לִקְבּוֹעַ מְזוּזָה "to fix the *mezuzah*."

Before separating *challah*, לְהַפְרִישׁ חַלָּה "to separate *challah*."

Grace for Little Children.

בְּרִיךְ רַחֲמָנָא מָרֵיהּ דְּהַאי פִּתָּא "Blessed be the Merciful, the Giver of this bread."

[1] See page 61.

PRINTED BY BALLANTYNE, HANSON AND CO.
EDINBURGH AND LONDON.

A CATALOGUE

OF

DICTIONARIES, GRAMMARS, READING-BOOKS

AND OTHER IMPORTANT WORKS

OF THE PRINCIPAL

EUROPEAN LANGUAGES,

PUBLISHED BY

KEGAN PAUL, TRENCH, TRÜBNER, & CO., Ltd.

1 PATERNOSTER SQUARE, AND 57 & 59 LUDGATE HILL.

CONTENTS.

	PAGE		PAGE		PAGE
ALBANIAN	1	HUNGARIAN	11	ROUMANIAN	13
ANGLO-SAXON	1	INTERNATIONAL		RUSSIAN	13
BASQUE	2	LANGUAGES	11	SERBIAN	14
DANO-NORWEGIAN	2	ITALIAN	11	SPANISH	14
DUTCH	2	LATIN	12	SWEDISH	15
ENGLISH	3	NORWEGIAN — *see*		TECHNICAL DIC-	
FRENCH	5	DANO-NORWEGIAN.		TIONARIES	15
FRISIAN	9	POLISH	12	TURKISH	16
GERMAN	9	PORTUGUESE	13	WELSH	16
GREEK	11				

ALBANIAN.

GRAMMAIRE ALBANAISE à l'Usage de ceux qui désirent Apprendre cette Langue sans l'Aide d'un Maître. Par P. W. Crown 8vo, cloth, pp. viii. and 170. 1887. Price 7s. 6d.

ANGLO-SAXON.

HARRISON and BASKERVILL.—A HANDY DICTIONARY OF ANGLO-SAXON POETRY. Based on Groschopp's Grein. Edited, Revised, and Corrected, with Grammatical Appendix, List of Irregular Verbs, and Brief Etymological Features. By JAMES A. HARRISON, Professor of English and Modern Languages in Washington and Lee University, Virginia; and W. M. BASKERVILL, Ph.D. Lips., Professor of English Language and Literature in Vanderbilt University, Nashville, Ten. Square 8vo, cloth, pp. 318. 1886. Price 12s.

MARCH.—A COMPARATIVE GRAMMAR OF THE ANGLO-SAXON LANGUAGE; in which its forms are illustrated by those of the Sanskrit, Greek, Latin, Gothic, Old Saxon, Old Friesic, Old Norse, and Old High-German. By FRANCIS A. MARCH, LL.D. Demy 8vo, cloth, pp. xi. and 253. 1877. Price 10s.

MARCH.—INTRODUCTION TO ANGLO-SAXON. An Anglo-Saxon Reader. With Philological Notes, a Brief Grammar, and a Vocabulary. By FRANCIS A. MARCH, LL.D. 8vo, cloth, pp. viii. and 166. 1870. Price 7s. 6d.

RASK.—GRAMMAR OF THE ANGLO-SAXON TONGUE, from the Danish of Erasmus Rask. By BENJAMIN THORPE. Third Edition, corrected and improved, with Plate. Post 8vo, cloth, pp. vi. and 191. 1879. Price 5s. 6d.

WRIGHT.—ANGLO-SAXON AND OLD ENGLISH VOCABULARIES. By THOMAS WRIGHT, M.A., F.S.A., Hon. M.R.S.L. Illustrating the Condition and Manners of our Forefathers, as well as the History of the forms of Elementary Education, and of the Languages Spoken in this Island from the Tenth Century to the Fifteenth. Second Edition, Edited and Collated by RICHARD PAUL WÜLCKER. Two vols. demy 8vo, pp. xx.-408, and iv.-486, cloth. 1884. 28s.

BASQUE.

VAN EYS.—OUTLINES OF BASQUE GRAMMAR. By W. J. VAN EYS. Crown 8vo, cloth, pp. xii. and 52. 1883. Price 3s. 6d.

DANO-NORWEGIAN.

*****BOJESEN.—A GUIDE TO THE DANISH LANGUAGE.** Designed for English Students. By Mrs. MARIA BOJESEN. 12mo, cl., pp. 250. 1863. Price 5s.

LARSEN.—DANISH-ENGLISH DICTIONARY. By L. LARSEN. Crown 8vo, cloth, pp. 646. 1880. Price 10s. 6d.

*****OTTÉ.—DANO-NORWEGIAN GRAMMAR:** A Manual for Students of Danish, based on the Ollendorffian System of teaching Languages, and adapted for self-instruction. By E. C. OTTÉ. Second Edition. Crown 8vo, cloth, pp. xix. and 337. 1884. Price 7s. 6d.

Key to ditto. Crown 8vo, cloth, pp. 84. Price 3s.

*****OTTÉ.—SIMPLIFIED GRAMMAR OF THE DANISH LANGUAGE.** By E. C. OTTÉ. Crown 8vo, cloth, pp. viii. and 66. 1884. Price 2s. 6d.

ROSING.—ENGLISH-DANISH DICTIONARY. By S. ROSING. Crown 8vo, cloth, pp. 722. 1883. Price 8s. 6d.

SMITH and HORNEMAN.—NORWEGIAN GRAMMAR; with a Glossary for Tourists. By M. SMITH and H. HORNEMAN. Post 8vo, cloth pp. 64. 1889. Price 2s.

DUTCH.

*****AHN.—A CONCISE GRAMMAR OF THE DUTCH LANGUAGE,** with Selections from the Best Authors in Prose and Poetry. After Dr. F. AHN's Method. Fourth Edition, thoroughly Revised and Enlarged by Dr. J. M. HOOGVLIET and Dr. KERN (of Leiden). 12mo, pp. viii. and 168, cloth. 1887. Price 3s. 6d.

KRAMERS.—NEW POCKET DICTIONARY OF THE ENGLISH-DUTCH AND DUTCH-ENGLISH LANGUAGES. Containing also in the First Part Pronunciation, and a Vocabulary of Proper Names, Geographical and Historical. By J. KRAMERS. 16mo, cl., pp. xiv. & 714. 1876. Price 4s.

PICARD.—A NEW POCKET DICTIONARY OF THE ENGLISH-DUTCH AND DUTCH-ENGLISH LANGUAGES. Remodelled and corrected from the Best Authorities. By A. PICARD. Fifth Edition, 16mo, cloth, pp. xiv. and 1186. 1877. Price 10s.

ENGLISH.

ANDERSON.—PRACTICAL MERCANTILE CORRESPONDENCE. A Collection of Modern Letters of Business, with Notes, Critical and Explanatory, and an Appendix, containing a Dictionary of Commercial Technicalities, *pro forma* Invoices, Account Sales, Bills of Lading, and Bills of Exchange; also an Explanation of the German Chain Rule. Thirtieth Edition, revised and enlarged. By WILLIAM ANDERSON. Crown 8vo, cloth, pp. xxxii. and 280. Price 3s. 6d.

BELL.—SOUNDS AND THEIR RELATIONS. A Complete Manual of Universal Alphabets, Illustrated by means of Visible Speech; and Exhibiting the Pronunciation of English, in Various Styles, and of other Languages and Dialects. By A. MELVILLE BELL, F.E.I.S., &c. 4to, cloth, pp. viii. and 102. 1881. Price 7s. 6d.

BELL.—THE FAULTS OF SPEECH; a Self-Corrector and Teachers' Manual. By A. MELVILLE BELL, F.E.I.S. 18mo, cloth, pp. vi. and 65. 1880. Price 2s. 6d.

BELL.—THE PRINCIPLES OF ELOCUTION, with Exercises and Notations for Pronunciation, Intonation, Emphasis, Gesture, and Emotional Expression. By A. MELVILLE BELL, F.E.I.S., &c. Fourth Revised and Enlarged Edition. 12mo, cloth, pp. 243. 1878. Price 7s. 6d.

BELL.—VISIBLE SPEECH. The Science of Universal Alphabetics; or, Self-Interpreting Physiological Letters for the Writing of all Languages in One Alphabet. Illustrated by Tables, Diagrams and Examples. By A. MELVILLE BELL, F.E.I.S., &c. 4to, cloth, pp. 126. 1867. Price £1, 5s.

**BELL.—ENGLISH VISIBLE SPEECH FOR THE MILLION for Communicating the Exact Pronunciation of the Language to Native and Foreign Learners, and for Teaching Children and Illiterate Adults to Read in a few days. By A. MELVILLE BELL, F.E.I.S., &c. 4to, paper, pp. 16. 1867. Price 2s.

FURNIVALL.—EDUCATION IN EARLY ENGLAND. Some Notes used as Forewords to a Collection of Treatises on "Manners and Meals in Olden Times," for the Early English Text Society. By FREDERICK J. FURNIVALL, M.A. 8vo, paper, pp. 4 and lxxiv. 1867. Price 1s.

GALLOWAY.—EDUCATION: SCIENTIFIC AND TECHNICAL; or, How the Inductive Sciences are Taught, and How they Ought to be Taught. By R. GALLOWAY, F.C.S. 8vo, cl., pp. xvi. & 462. 1881. Price 10s. 6d.

GOULD.—GOOD ENGLISH; or, Popular Errors in Language. By EDWARD S. GOULD. New Edition. Crown 8vo, cloth, pp. ix. and 214. 1880. Price 6s.

HALL.—ON ENGLISH ADJECTIVES IN -ABLE, with Special Reference to RELIABLE. By FITZEDWARD HALL, C.E., M.A., Hon. D.C.L., Oxon. Crown 8vo, cloth, pp. viii. and 238. 1877. Price 7s. 6d.

HARLEY.—THE SIMPLIFICATION OF ENGLISH SPELLING, specially adapted to the Rising Generation. An Easy Way of Saving Time in Writing, Printing, and Reading. By Dr. GEORGE HARLEY, F.R.S., F.C.S. 8vo, cloth, pp. 128. 1877. Price 2s. 6d.

HYMANS.—PUPIL versus TEACHER. Letters from a Teacher to a Teacher. By M. HYMANS. 18mo, cloth, pp. 92. 1875. Price 2s.

INMAN.—HISTORY OF THE ENGLISH ALPHABET. A Paper read before the Liverpool Literary and Philosophical Society. By T. INMAN, M.D. 8vo, paper, pp. 36. 1872. Price 1s.

JENKINS.—VEST-POCKET LEXICON. An English Dictionary of all except Familiar Words, including the principal Scientific and Technical Terms, and Foreign Moneys, Weights and Measures; omitting what everybody knows, and containing what everybody wants to know and cannot readily find. By JABEZ JENKINS. 64mo, cloth, pp. 563. 1890. Price 1s.

MANNING.—AN INQUIRY INTO THE CHARACTER AND ORIGIN OF THE POSSESSIVE AUGMENT in English and in Cognate Dialects. By the late JAMES MANNING, Q.A.S., Recorder of Oxford. 8vo, paper, pp. iv. and 90. 1864. Price 2s.

PARRY.—A SHORT CHAPTER ON LETTER-CHANGE, with Examples. Being chiefly an attempt to reduce in a simple manner the principal classical and cognate words to their primitive meanings. By J. PARRY, B.A., formerly Scholar of Corpus Christi College, Cambridge. Fcap. 8vo, pp. 16, wrapper. 1884. Price 1s.

PLUMPTRE.—KING'S COLLEGE LECTURES ON ELOCUTION; or, The Physiology and Culture of Voice and Speech, and the Expression of the Emotions by Language, Countenance and Gesture. To which is added a Special Lecture on the Causes and Cure of the Impediments of Speech. Being the Substance of the Introductory Course of Lectures annually delivered by CHARLES JOHN PLUMPTRE, Lecturer on Public Reading and Speaking at King's College, London, in the Evening Classes Department. Dedicated by permission to H. R. H. the Prince of Wales. Fourth and greatly enlarged Illustrated Edition. 8vo, cloth, pp. xvi. and 494. 1883. Price 15s.

PLUMPTRE.—THE RIGHT MODE OF RESPIRATION, in Regard to Speech, Song, and Health. By CHARLES JOHN PLUMPTRE, Author of "King's College Lectures on Elocution," of which this forms Lecture VI. Demy 8vo, pp. iv.-16, wrapper. Price 1s.

RUNDALL.—A SHORT AND EASY WAY TO WRITE ENGLISH AS SPOKEN. By J. B. RUNDALL, Certificated Member of the London Shorthand Writers' Association. Price 6d.

SPRUNER.—HISTORICO-GEOGRAPHICAL HAND-ATLAS By Dr. KARL VON SPRUNER. Third Edition. Twenty-seven Coloured Maps. Oblong cloth. 1872. Price 15s.

TURNER.—THE ENGLISH LANGUAGE. A Concise History of the English Language, with a Glossary showing the Derivation and Pronunciation of the English Words. By ROGER TURNER. In German and English on opposite Pages. 18mo, pp. viii.-80, sewed. 1884. Price 1s. 6d.

UNGER.—SHORT CUT TO READING. The Child's First Book of Lessons. Part I. By W. H. UNGER. Seventh Edition. Crown 8vo, cloth, pp. 32. 1878. Price 5d. *In folio sheets*, pp. 44. Sets A to D, 10d. each; set E, 8d. *Complete*, 4s. SEQUEL to Part I. and Part II. Sixth Edition. Crown 8vo, cloth, pp. 64. 1877. Price 6d. Parts I. and II. in One Volume. Third Edition. Demy 8vo, cloth, pp. 76. 1873. Price 1s. 6d.

UNGER.—CONTINUOUS SUPPLEMENTARY WRITING MODELS, designed to impart not only a Good Business Hand, but Correctness in Transcribing. By W. H. UNGER. New Edition. Oblong 8vo, stiff covers, pp. 44. Price 6d.

UNGER.—THE STUDENT'S BLUE BOOK. Being Selections from Official Correspondence, Reports, &c.; for Exercises in Reading and Copying Manuscripts, Writing, Orthography, Punctuation, Dictation, Précis, Indexing, and Digesting, and Tabulating Accounts and Returns. Compiled by W. H. UNGER. Folio, paper, pp. 100. 1875. Price 2s.

UNGER.—TWO HUNDRED TESTS IN ENGLISH ORTHOGRAPHY, or Word Dictations. Compiled by W. H. UNGER. Fcap. 8vo, cloth, pp. vi. and 200. 1877. Price 1s. 6d. ; interleaved, 2s. 6d.

UNGER.—THE SCRIPT PRIMER. By which one of the Remaining Difficulties of Children is entirely removed in the First Stages, and, as a consequence, a considerable saving of time will be effected. In Two Parts. By W. H. UNGER. Part I. 12mo, cloth, pp. xv. and 44. 1879. Price 5d. Part II. 12mo, cloth, pp. 59. 1879. Price 5d.

UNGER.—PRELIMINARY WORD DICTATIONS ON THE RULES FOR SPELLING. By W. H. UNGER. 18mo, cloth, pp. 44. Price 4d.; interleaved, 6d.

WEDGWOOD.—THE PRINCIPLES OF GEOMETRICAL DEMONSTRATION, reduced from the Original Conception of Space and Form. By H. WEDGWOOD, M.A. 12mo, cloth, pp. 48. 1844. Price 2s.

WEDGWOOD.—ON THE DEVELOPMENT OF THE UNDERSTANDING. By H. WEDGWOOD, M.A. 12mo, cloth, pp. 133. 1848. Price 3s.

WEDGWOOD.—THE GEOMETRY OF THE THREE FIRST BOOKS OF EUCLID. By Direct Proof from Definitions alone. By H. WEDGWOOD, M.A. 12mo, cloth, pp. 104. 1856. Price 3s.

WEDGWOOD.—ON THE ORIGIN OF LANGUAGE. By H. WEDGWOOD, M.A. 12mo, cloth. pp. 165. 1866. Price 3s. 6d.

WEDGWOOD.—A DICTIONARY OF ENGLISH ETYMOLOGY. By H. WEDGWOOD, M.A. Third Edition, revised and enlarged. With Introduction on the Origin of Language. Fourth Edition. 8vo, cloth, pp. lxxii. and 746. 1888. Price £1, 1s.

WEDGWOOD.—CONTESTED ETYMOLOGIES IN THE DICTIONARY OF THE REV. W. W. SKEAT. By H. WEDGWOOD. Crown 8vo, cloth, pp. viii.-194. 1882. Price 5s.

WIEBÉ.—THE PARADISE OF CHILDHOOD. A Manual for Self-Instruction in Friederich Froebel's Educational Principles, and a Pract'cal Guide to Kinder-Gartners. By EDWARD WIEBÉ. With Seventy-four Plates of Illustrations. 4to, paper, pp. iv.-83. 1869. Price 7s. 6d.

WITHERS.—THE ENGLISH LANGUAGE SPELLED AS PRONOUNCED. with Enlarged Alphabet of Forty Letters, a Letter for each Distinct Element in the Language. By G. WITHERS. 8vo, paper, pp. 77. 1874. Price 1s.

FRENCH.

*AHN.—NEW, PRACTICAL, AND EASY METHOD OF LEARNING THE FRENCH LANGUAGE. By Dr. F. AHN. First Course. 12mo, cloth, pp. 114. Price 1s. 6d. Second Course. 12mo, cloth, pp. 170. Price 1s. 6d. The Two Courses in 1 vol. 12mo, cloth. 1879. Price 3s.

*AHN.—NEW, PRACTICAL, AND EASY METHOD OF LEARNING THE FRENCH LANGUAGE. Third Course, containing a French Reader, with Notes and Vocabulary. By H. W. EHRLICH. 12mo, cloth, pp. viii. and 125. 1890. Price 1s. 6d.

*ARAGO.—LES ARISTOCRATIES. A Comedy in Verse. By ÉTIENNE ARAGO. Edited, with English Notes and Notice on Étienne Arago, by the Rev. P. H. E. BRETTE, B.D., Head-Master of the French School, Christ's Hospital, Examiner in the University of London. 12mo, cloth, pp. xiii. and 235. 1869. Price 4s.

ASPLET.—THE COMPLETE FRENCH COURSE. Part II. Containing all the Rules of French Syntax, Irregular Verbs, Adjectives, and Verbs, together with Extracts from the Best Authors. By GEORGES C. ASPLET, French Master, Frome. 12mo, cloth, pp. xviii. and 276. 1880. Price 2s. 6d.

*AUGIER.—DIANE. A Drama in Verse. By ÉMILE AUGIER. Edited, with English Notes and Notice on Augier, by THEODORE KARCHER, LL.B., of the Royal Military Academy and the University of London. 12mo, cloth, pp. xiii. and 145. 1867. Price 2s. 6d.

BARANOWSKI.—VADE-MECUM DE LA LANGUE FRANCAISE. Rédigé d'après les Dictionnaires classiques avec les Exemples de Bonnes Locutions que donne l'Académie Française, on qu'on trouve dans les ouvrages des plus célèbres auteurs. Par J. J. BARANOWSKI, avec l'approbation de M. E. LITTRÉ, Sénateur, &c. 32mo, cloth, pp. x.–223. 1879. Price 2s. 6d.; morocco, 3s. 6d.; morocco tuck, 4s.

*BARRIERE and CAPENDU.—LES FAUX BONSHOMMES. A Comedy. By THÉODORE BARRIÈRE and ERNEST CAPENDU. Edited, with English Notes and Notice on Barrière, by Professor CH. CASSAL, LL.D., of University College, London. 12mo, cloth, pp. xvi. and 304. 1868. Price 4s.

BELLOWS.—TOUS LES VERBES. Conjugations of all the Verbs in the French and English Languages. By JOHN BELLOWS. Revised by Professor BELJAME, B.A., LL.B., and GEORGE B. STRICKLAND, late Assistant French Master, Royal Naval School, London. Also a New Table of Equivalent Values of French and English Money, Weights, and Measures. Second Edition. 32mo, sewed, pp. 48. 1889. Price 6d.

BELLOWS.—DICTIONARY FOR THE POCKET. French and English— English and French. Both divisions on same page. By JOHN BELLOWS. Masculine and Feminine Words shown by distinguishing Types, Conjugations of all the Verbs, *Liaison* marked in French Part, and Hints to Aid Pronunciation, together with Tables and Maps. Revised by ALEXANDRE BELJAME, M.A. Second Edition. 32mo, roan tuck, pp. 608. 1880. Price 10s. 6d.; morocco tuck, 12s. 6d.

BRETTE and THOMAS.—FRENCH EXAMINATION PAPERS, set at the University of London from 1839 to January 1888. Compiled and edited by the Rev. P. H. ERNEST BRETTE, B.D., Head Master of the French School, Christ's Hospital, London; Examiner in the University of London; at Eton College, &c., &c.; and FERDINAND THOMAS, B.A., B.Sc., Late Assistant Examiner in the University of London.

PART I.—MATRICULATION EXAMINATIONS, JULY 1853 TO JANUARY 1888. Crown 8vo, cloth, pp. xx. and 176. Price 3s. 6d.

KEY TO PART I. Price 5s.

In the Key all the Extracts from the Writings of French Authors are translated into English, and all the Questions on Grammar, Idiom, and Elementary Etymology are fully answered.

PART II.—FIRST B.A. (or INTERMEDIATE IN ARTS) and B.A. PASS EXAMINATIONS;—Examinations for Honours (Intermediate in Arts and B.A.); and for Certificates of Higher Proficiency—M.A. (Branch IV.), and D.Litt. Examinations. Crown 8vo, cloth, pp. xx. and 441. Price 7s.

The KEY TO PART II. will be divided into Two Divisions, and will be published early in 1890.

CASSAL.—GLOSSARY OF IDIOMS, GALLICISMS, and other Difficulties contained in the Senior Course of the Modern French Reader. With Short Notices of the most important French Writers and Historical or Literary Characters, and Hints as to the Works to be Read or Studied. By CHARLES CASSAL, LL.D. 12mo, cloth, pp. viii. and 104. 1880. Price 2s. 6d.

*****EHRLICH.—FRENCH READER.** With Notes and Vocabulary. By H. W. EHRLICH. 12mo, limp cloth, pp. viii. and 125. 1877. Price 1s. 6d.

FRUSTON.—ECHO FRANCAIS. A Practical Guide to French Conversation. By F. DE LA FRUSTON. With a Complete Vocabulary. Second Edition. Crown 8vo, cloth, pp. 120 and 71. 1878. Price 3s.

*****KARCHER.—QUESTIONNAIRE FRANCAIS.** Questions on French Grammar, Idiomatic Difficulties, and Military Expressions. By THEODORE KARCHER, LL.B. Fourth Edition, greatly enlarged. Crown 8vo, cloth, pp. viii. and 215. 1879. Price 4s. 6d. ; interleaved with writing paper, 5s. 6d.

*****LE-BRUN.—MATERIALS FOR TRANSLATING FROM ENGLISH INTO FRENCH.** Being a Short Essay on Translation, followed by a Graduated Selection in Prose and Verse. By L. LE-BRUN. Sixth Edition. Revised and corrected by HENRI VAN LAUN. Crown 8vo, cloth, pp. xii. and 204. 1882. Price 4s. 6d.

*****LITTLE FRENCH READER (The).** Extracted from "The Modern French Reader." Edited by Professor C. CASSAL, LL.B., and Professor T. KARCHER, LL.B. With a New System of Conjugating the French Verbs, by Professor CASSAL. Fourth Edition. Crown 8vo, cloth, pp. 112. 1884. Price 2s.

MANESCA.—THE SERIAL AND ORAL METHOD OF TEACHING LANGUAGES. Adapted to the French. By L. MANESCA. New Edition, carefully revised. Crown 8vo, cloth, pp. xxviii. and 535. Price 7s. 6d.

*****MARMONTEL.—BÉLISAIRE.** Par J. F. MARMONTEL. With Introduction by the Rev. P. H. E. BRETTE and Professors CASSAL and KARCHER. Nouvelle Edition, 12mo, cloth, pp. xii. and 123. 1867. Price 2s. 6d.

*****MODERN FRENCH READER (The). PROSE. Junior Course.** Edited by C. CASSAL, LL.D., and THEODORE KARCHER, LL.B. Eighth Edition. Crown 8vo, cloth, pp. xiv. and 224. 1890. Price 2s. 6d.

*****MODERN FRENCH READER (The). PROSE. Senior Course.** Edited by C. CASSAL, LL.D., and THEODORE KARCHER, LL.B. Third Edition. Crown 8vo, cl., pp. xi. & 418. 1880. Price 4s. With Glossary. Price 6s.

NOIRIT.—A FRENCH COURSE IN TEN LESSONS. By JULES NOIRIT, B.A. Lessons I.-IV. Crown 8vo, limp cloth, pp. xiv. and 80. 1870. Price 1s. 6d.

NOIRIT.—FRENCH GRAMMATICAL QUESTIONS for the Use of Gentlemen Preparing for the Army, Civil Service, Oxford Examinations, &c., &c. By JULES NOIRIT. Crown 8vo, cloth, pp. 62. 1870. Price 1s.; interleaved, 1s. 6d.

NOTLEY.—COMPARATIVE GRAMMAR OF THE FRENCH, ITALIAN, SPANISH, AND PORTUGUESE LANGUAGES. With a Copious Vocabulary. By EDWIN A. NOTLEY. Oblong 12mo, cloth, pp. xv. and 396. 1868. Price 7s. 6d.

**NUGENT'S IMPROVED FRENCH AND ENGLISH AND ENGLISH AND
FRENCH POCKET DICTIONARY.** Par SMITH. 24mo, cloth, pp. xxxii.
and 320, and 488. 1875. Price 3s.

*****PONSARD.—CHARLOTTE CORDAY.** A Tragedy. By F. PONSARD.
Edited, with English Notes and Notice on Ponsard, by Professor C.
CASSAL, LL.D. Third Edition. 12mo, cloth, pp. xi. and 133. 1871.
Price 2s. 6d.

*****PONSARD.—L'HONNEUR ET L'ARGENT.** A Comedy. By F. PONSARD.
Edited, with English Notes and Memoir of Ponsard, by Professor C.
CASSAL, LL.D. Second Edition. 12mo, cloth, pp. xvi. and 171.
1869. Price 3s. 6d.

ROCHE.—FRENCH GRAMMAR for the Use of English Students, adopted
for the Public Schools by the Imperial Council of Public Instruction.
By A. ROCHE. Crown 8vo, cloth, pp. xii. and 176. 1869. Price 3s.

ROCHE.—PROSE AND POETRY. Select Pieces from the Best English
Authors, for Reading, Composition, and Translation. By A. ROCHE.
Second Edition. Fcap. 8vo, cl., pp. viii. and 226. 1872. Price 2s. 6d.

RUNDALL.—MÉTHODE RAPIDE ET FACILE D'ÉCRIRE LE FRANCAIS
COMME ON LE PARLE. Par J. B. RUNDALL. Price 6d.

*****THÉÂTRE FRANCAIS MODERNE.—A Selection of Modern French Plays.**
Edited by the Rev. P. H. E. BRETTE, B.D.; C. CASSAL, LL.D.; and
TH. KARCHER, LL.B.

First Series, in 1 vol. crown 8vo, cloth. Price 6s. Containing—
>   CHARLOTTE CORDAY. A Tragedy. By F. PONSARD. Edited,
>   with English Notes and Notice on Ponsard, by Professor C.
>   CASSAL, LL.D.
>
>   DIANE. A Drama in Verse. By EMILE AUGIER. Edited, with
>   English Notes and Notice on Augier, by TH. KARCHER, LL.B.
>
>   LE VOYAGE À DIEPPE. A Comedy in Prose. By WAFFLARD and
>   FULGENCE. Edited, with English Notes, by the Rev. P. H. E.
>   BRETTE, B.D.

Second Series, crown 8vo, cloth. Price 6s. Containing—
>   MOLIÈRE. A Drama in Prose. By GEORGE SAND. Edited, with
>   English Notes and Notice of George Sand, by TH. KARCHER, LL.B.
>
>   LES ARISTOCRATIES. A Comedy in Verse. By ÉTIENNE ARAGO.
>   Edited, with English Notes and Notice of Étienne Arago, by
>   the Rev. P. H. E. BRETTE, B.D.

Third Series, crown 8vo, cloth. Price 6s. Containing—
>   LES FAUX BONSHOMMES. A Comedy. By THÉODORE BARRIÈRE
>   and ERNEST CAPENDU. Edited, with English Notes and
>   Notice on Barrière, by Professor C. CASSAL, LL.D.
>
>   L'HONNEUR ET L'ARGENT. A Comedy. By F. PONSARD. Edited,
>   with English Notes and Memoir of Ponsard, by Professor C.
>   CASSAL, LL.D.

*VAN LAUN.—GRAMMAR OF THE FRENCH LANGUAGE. In Three Parts. Parts I. and II. Accidence and Syntax. By H. VAN LAUN. Nineteenth Edition. Crown 8vo, cloth, pp. 151 and 120. 1880. Price 4s. Part III. Exercises. Eighteenth Edition. Crown 8vo, cloth, pp. xii. and 285. 1880. Price 3s. 6d.

*WAFFLARD and FULGENCE.—LE VOYAGE À DIEPPE. A Comedy in Prose. By MM. WAFFLARD and FULGENCE. Edited, with English Notes, by the Rev. P. H. E. BRETTE, B.D. Second Edition, revised, with an Index to the Notes. 12mo, cloth, pp. 107. 1870. Price 2s. 6d.

WELLER.—AN IMPROVED DICTIONARY. English and French, and French and English, including Technical, Scientific, Legal, Commercial, Naval, and Military Terms, Vocabularies of Engineering, &c., Railway Terms, Steam Navigation, Geographical Names, Ancient Mythology, Classical Antiquity, and Christian Names in present use. By E. WELLER. Third Edition. Royal 8vo, cloth, pp. 384 and 340. 1864. Price 7s. 6d.

FRISIAN.

CUMMINS.—GRAMMAR OF THE OLD FRIESIC LANGUAGE. By A. H. CUMMINS, A.M. Crown 8vo, pp. 128, cloth. 1887. Price 6s.

GERMAN.

*AHN.—PRACTICAL GRAMMAR OF THE GERMAN LANGUAGE, with a Grammatical Index and Glossary of all the German Words. By Dr. F. AHN. A New Edition, containing numerous Additions, Alterations, and Improvements. By DAWSON W. TURNER, D.C.L., and Prof. F. L. WEINMANN. Crown 8vo, cloth, pp. cxi. and 430. 1878. Price 3s. 6d.

*AHN.—NEW, PRACTICAL, AND EASY METHOD OF LEARNING THE GERMAN LANGUAGE. By Dr. F. AHN. First and Second Course, in 1 volume, 12mo, cloth, pp. 86 and 120. 1880. Price 3s.
KEY to Ditto. 12mo, sewed, pp. 40. Price 8d.

*AHN.—MANUAL OF GERMAN CONVERSATION, or Vade Mecum for English Travellers. By Dr. F. AHN. Second Edition. 12mo, cloth, pp. x. and 137. 1875. Price 1s. 6d.

*APEL.—PROSE SPECIMENS FOR TRANSLATION INTO GERMAN, with copious Vocabularies. By H. APEL. 12mo, cloth, pp. viii. and 246, 1862. Price 4s. 6d.

*BENEDIX.—DER VETTER. Comedy in Three Acts. By Roderich Benedix. With Grammatical and Explanatory Notes by F. WEINMANN, German Master at the Royal Institution School, Liverpool, and G. ZIMMERMANN, Teacher of Modern Languages. 12mo, cloth, pp. 126. 1863. Price 2s. 6d.

BOLIA.—THE GERMAN CALIGRAPHIST. Copies for German Handwriting. By C. BOLIA. Obl. fcap. 4to, sewed, pp. 6. Price 1s.

DUSAR.—GRAMMAR OF THE GERMAN LANGUAGE; with Exercises. By P. FRIEDRICH DUSAR, First German Master in the Military Department of Cheltenham College. Second Edition. Crown 8vo, cloth, pp. viii. and 207. 1879. Price 4s. 6d.

DUSAR.—GRAMMATICAL COURSE OF THE GERMAN LANGUAGE.
By P. FRIEDRICH DUSAR. Second Edition. Crown 8vo, cloth, pp. x. and 134. 1877. Price 3s. 6d.

FRIEDRICH.—PROGRESSIVE GERMAN READER. With Copious Notes to the First Part. By P. FRIEDRICH. Second Edition. Crown 8vo, cloth, pp. vii. and 190. 1876. Price 4s. 6d.

*FRŒMBLING.—GRADUATED GERMAN READER. Consisting of a Selection from the most Popular Writers, arranged progressively; with a complete Vocabulary for the First Part. By FRIEDRICH OTTO FRŒMBLING, Ph.D. Eighth Edition. 12mo, cloth, pp. viii. and 306. 1879. Price 3s. 6d.

*FRŒMBLING.—GRADUATED EXERCISES FOR TRANSLATION INTO GERMAN. Consisting of Extracts from the best English Authors, arranged progressively; with an Appendix, containing Idiomatic Notes. By FRIEDRICH OTTO FRŒMBLING, Ph.D., Principal German Master at the City of London School. Crown 8vo, cloth, pp. xiv. and 322. With Notes, pp. 66. 1867. Price 4s. 6d. Without Notes, 4s.

LANGE.—GERMAN PROSE WRITING. Comprising English Passages for Translation into German. Selected from Examination Papers of the University of London, the College of Preceptors, London, and the Royal Military Academy, Woolwich, arranged progressively, with Notes and Theoretical as well as Practical Treatises on Themes for the Writing of Essays. By F. K. W. LANGE, Ph.D., Assistant German Master, Royal Academy, Woolwich; Examiner, Royal College of Preceptors, London. Crown 8vo, pp. viii. and 176, cloth. 1881. Price 4s.

LANGE.—GERMANIA. A German Reading-Book, arranged Progressively. By FRANZ K. W. LANGE, Ph.D. Part I.—Anthology of German Prose and Poetry, with Vocabulary and Biographical Notes. 8vo, cloth, pp. xvi. and 216. 1881. Price 3s. 6d. Part II.—Essays on German History and Institutions. With Notes. 8vo, cloth, pp. 124. Parts I. and II. together. 1881. Price 5s. 6d.

LANGE.—GERMAN GRAMMAR PRACTICE. By F. K. W. LANGE, Ph.D., &c. Crown 8vo, pp. viii. and 64, cloth. 1882. Price 1s. 6d.

LANGE.—COLLOQUIAL GERMAN GRAMMAR. With Special Reference to the Anglo-Saxon Element in the English Language. By F. K. W. LANGE, Ph.D., &c. Crown 8vo, pp. xxxii. and 380, cloth. 1882. Price 4s. 6d.

RUNDALL.—KURZE UND LEICHTE WEISE DEUTSCH ZU SCHREIBEN wie man es Spricht. Von J. B. Rundall. Price 6d.

SINCLAIR.—A GERMAN VOCABULARY OF SOME OF THE MINOR DIFFICULTIES IN THE GERMAN LANGUAGE, AND EASY CONVERSATIONS. By F. SINCLAIR. Crown 8vo, cloth, pp. 88. 1888. Price 2s.

WOLFRAM.—DEUTSCHES ECHO. The German Echo. A Faithful Mirror of German Conversation. By LUDWIG WOLFRAM. With a Vocabulary, by HENRY P. SKELTON. Sixth Revised Edition. Crown 8vo, cloth, pp. 128 and 69. 1879. Price 3s.

GREEK.

**CONTOPOULOS. — A LEXICON OF MODERN GREEK-ENGLISH AND
ENGLISH MODERN GREEK.** By N. CONTOPOULOS. Part I. Modern Greek-English. Part II. English Modern Greek. In 2 vols. 8vo, cloth, pp. 460 and 582. 1877. Price 27s.

**CONTOPOULOS.—HANDBOOK OF ENGLISH AND GREEK DIALOGUES
AND CORRESPONDENCE,** with a Short Guide to the Antiquities of Athens. By N. CONTOPOULOS. Crown 8vo, cloth, pp. 238. Price 2s. 6d.

*GELDART.—A GUIDE TO MODERN GREEK. By E. M. GELDART, M.A. Post 8vo, cloth, pp. xii. and 274. 1883. Price 7s. 6d.—KEY, cloth, pp. 28, price 2s. 6d.

*GELDART.—SIMPLIFIED GRAMMAR OF MODERN GREEK. By E. M. GELDART, M.A. Crown 8vo, cloth, pp. 68. 1883. Price 2s. 6d.

**LASCARIDES. — A COMPREHENSIVE PHRASEOLOGICAL ENGLISH-
ANCIENT AND MODERN GREEK LEXICON.** Founded upon a Manuscript of G. P. LASCARIDES, Esq., and compiled by L. MYRIANTHEUS, Ph.D. Two vols., cloth, fcap. 8vo, pp. xii. and 1338. 1883. Price £1, 10s.

HUNGARIAN.

*SINGER.—A SIMPLIFIED GRAMMAR OF THE HUNGARIAN LANGUAGE. By IGNATIUS SINGER, of Buda-Pesth. Crown 8vo, pp. vi. and 88, cloth. 1882. Price 4s. 6d.

INTERNATIONAL LANGUAGES.

BELL.—WORLD ENGLISH THE UNIVERSAL LANGUAGE. By ALEXANDER MELVILLE BELL, Author of "Visible Speech," &c. Royal 8vo, pp. 34, wrappers. 1888. Price 1s.

BELL.—HANDBOOK OF WORLD ENGLISH. By ALEXANDER MELVILLE BELL, Author of "Visible Speech," &c. Demy 8vo, pp. 38 wrappers, cloth back. 1888. Price 1s.

**SPRAGUE.—THE INTERNATIONAL LANGUAGE. HANDBOOK OF VOLA-
PÜK.** By CHARLES E. SPRAGUE, Member of the Academy of Volapük, President of the Institute of Accounts, U.S. Crown 8vo, cloth, pp. viii. and 119. Price 5s.

WOOD. — DICTIONARY OF VOLAPUK. Volapuk-English and English-Volapuk. By M. M. WOOD, M.D., Captain and Assistant-Surgeon, United States Army, Volapükatidel e cif. Crown 8vo, cloth, pp. viii. and 398. 1889. Price 10s. 6d. Volapuk has obtained a footing of its own among the speakers of twenty-one different tongues, and its adherents are numbered by hundreds of thousands.

ITALIAN.

***AHN.—NEW, PRACTICAL, AND EASY METHOD OF LEARNING THE
ITALIAN LANGUAGE.** By Dr. F. AHN. First and Second Course. Thirteenth Issue. 12mo, cloth, pp. iv. and 198. 1886. Price 3s. 6d.

CAMERINI.—L'ECO ITALIANO. A Practical Guide to Italian Conversation. By EUGENE CAMERINI. With a Complete Vocabulary. Second Edition. Crown 8vo, cloth, pp. viii., 128, and 98. 1871. Price 4s. 6d.

LANARI.—COLLECTION OF ITALIAN AND ENGLISH DIALOGUES ON GENERAL SUBJECTS. For the Use of those Desirous of Speaking the Italian Language Correctly. Preceded by a Brief Treatise on the Pronunciation of the same. By A. LANARI. 12mo, cloth, pp. viii. and 199. Price 3s. 6s.

MILLHOUSE.—MANUAL OF ITALIAN CONVERSATION, for the Use of Schools and Travellers. By JOHN MILLHOUSE. New Edition. 18mo, cloth, pp. 126. 1879. Price 2s.

MILLHOUSE. — NEW ENGLISH AND ITALIAN PRONOUNCING AND EXPLANATORY DICTIONARY. By JOHN MILLHOUSE. Vol. I. English-Italian. Vol. II. Italian-English. Sixth Edition. 2 vols. square 8vo, cloth, pp. 654 and 740. 1887. Price 12s.

NOTLEY. — COMPARATIVE GRAMMAR OF THE FRENCH, ITALIAN, SPANISH, AND PORTUGUESE LANGUAGES. With a Copious Vocabulary. By EDWIN A. NOTLEY. Oblong 12mo, cloth, pp. xv. and 396. 1868. Price 7s. 6d.

TOSCANI.—ITALIAN CONVERSATIONAL COURSE. A New Method of Teaching the Italian Language, both Theoretically and Practically. By GIOVANNI TOSCANI, late Professor of the Italian Language and Literature in Queen's College, London, &c. Fifth Edition. 12mo, cloth, pp. xiv. and 300. 1880. Price 5s.

TOSCANI.—ITALIAN READING COURSE. Comprehending Specimens in Prose and Poetry of the most distinguished Italian Writers, with Biographical Notices, Explanatory Notes, and Rules on Prosody. By G. TOSCANI. 12mo, cloth, pp. xii. and 160. With Table of Verbs. 1875. Price 4s. 6d.

LATIN.

*IHNE.—LATIN GRAMMAR FOR BEGINNERS, on Ahn's System. By W. H. IHNE, late Principal of Carlton Terrace School, Liverpool. Crown 8vo, cloth, pp. vi. and 184. 1864. Price 3s.

LEWIS.—JUVENALIS SATIRÆ. With a Literal English Prose Translation and Notes. By J. D. LEWIS, M.A., Trinity College, Cambridge. Second Edition. 2 vols. 8vo, cloth, pp. xii. and 230 and 400. 1882. Price 12s.

LEWIS.—THE LETTERS OF PLINY THE YOUNGER. Translated by J. D. LEWIS, M.A., Trinity College, Cambridge. Post 8vo, cloth, pp. vii. and 390. 1879. Price 5s.

POLISH.

BARANOWSKI.—SLOWNIK POLSKO-ANGIELSKI OPRACOWANY. Przez J. J. BARANOWSKIEGO, 6 Podsekretarza Banku Polskiego, w Warszawie. (Polish-English Lexicon. With Grammatical Rules in Polish.) 16mo, cloth, pp. 403. Price 12s.

BARANOWSKI.—ANGLO-POLISH LEXICON. By J. J. BARANOWSKI, formerly Under-Secretary to the Bank of Poland, in Warsaw. (With Grammatical Rules in English, and a Second Part, containing Dialogues, Bills of Exchange, Receipts, Letters, &c.; English and Polish Proverbs, &c.) 16mo, cloth, pp. vii. 400 and 90. Price 12s.

*MORFILL.—SIMPLIFIED GRAMMAR OF THE POLISH LANGUAGE. By W. R. MORFILL, M.A. Cr. 8vo, pp. viii.-64, cloth. 1884. Price 3s. 6d.

PORTUGUESE.

*ANDERSON and TUGMAN.—MERCANTILE CORRESPONDENCE. Containing a Collection of Commercial Letters in Portuguese and English, with their Translation on opposite pages, for the Use of Business Men and of Students in either of the Languages, treating in Modern Style of the System of Business in the principal Commercial Cities of the World. Accompanied by *pro forma* Accounts, Sales, Invoices, Bills of Lading, Drafts, &c. With an Introduction and Copious Notes. By WILLIAM ANDERSON and JAMES E. TUGMAN. 12mo, cloth, pp. xi. and 193. 1867. Price 6s.

BENSABAT. — NOVO DICCIONARIO INGLEZ - PORTUGUEZ. Composte sobre os Diccionarios de Johnson, Webster, Grand, Richardson, &c., e as Obras especiales de uma e outra Lingua por JACOB BENSABAT. 8vo, sheep, pp. xvi. and 1596. 1883. Price £1, 10s.

*D'ORSEY.—PRACTICAL GRAMMAR OF PORTUGUESE AND ENGLISH. Exhibiting in a Series of Exercises, in Double Translation, the Idiomatic Structure of both Languages, as now written and spoken. By the Rev. ALEXANDER J. D. D'ORSEY, B.D., of Corpus Christi College, Cambridge, and Lecturer on Public Reading and Speaking at King's College, London. Fourth Edition. Crown 8vo, cloth, pp. viii. and 302. 1887. Price 7s.

*D'ORSEY.—COLLOQUIAL PORTUGUESE; or, Words and Phrases of Everyday Life. Compiled from Dictation and Conversation. For the Use of English Tourists in Portugal, Brazil, Madeira, and the Azores. With a Brief Collection of Epistolary Phrases. By the Rev. A. J. D. D'ORSEY. Fourth Edition, enlarged. Crown 8vo, cloth, pp. viii. and 126. 1886. Price 3s. 6d.

NOTLEY. — COMPARATIVE GRAMMAR OF THE FRENCH, ITALIAN SPANISH, AND PORTUGUESE LANGUAGES. With a Copious Vocabulary By EDWIN A. NOTLEY. Oblong 12mo, cloth, pp. xv. and 396. 1868 Price 7s. 6d.

VIEYRA.—A NEW POCKET DICTIONARY OF THE PORTUGUESE AND ENGLISH LANGUAGES. In Two Parts, Portuguese and English and English and Portuguese. Abridged from "Vieyra's Dictionary." A New Edition, considerably Enlarged and Corrected. Two vols. Pott 8vo, pp. viii. and 760 and vi. and 924, bound in leather. 1889. Price 10s.

ROUMANIAN.

*TORCEANU.—SIMPLIFIED GRAMMAR OF THE ROUMANIAN LANGUAGE. By R. TORCEANU. Crown 8vo, cloth, pp. viii. and 72. 1884. Price 5s.

RUSSIAN.

ALEXANDROW. — COMPLETE ENGLISH-RUSSIAN AND RUSSIAN-ENGLISH DICTIONARY. By A. ALEXANDROW. 2 vols. demy 8vo, cloth. pp. x. and 734 and iv. and 1076. 1879 and 1885. Price £2.

FREETH.—A CONDENSED RUSSIAN GRAMMAR for the Use of Staff-Officers and Others. By F. FREETH, B.A., late Classical Scholar of Emmanuel College, Cambridge. Crown 8vo, pp. iv.-75, cloth. 1886. Price 3s. 6d.

MAKAROFF.—DICTIONNAIRE FRANCAIS-RUSSE ET RUSSE-FRANCAIS. Complet. Composé par N. P. MAKAROFF. Honoré par l'Académie des Sciences d'une Mention Honorable, approuvé par les Comités Scientifiques et adopté dans les Établissements d'Instruction. 2 vols. in four parts. Super royal 8vo, wrapper. 1884. Price 30s.

*RIOLA.—HOW TO LEARN RUSSIAN. A Manual for Students of Russian, based upon the Ollendorffian System of Teaching Languages, and adapted for Self-Instruction. By HENRY RIOLA, Teacher of the Russian Language. With a Preface by W. R. S. RALSTON, M.A. Fourth Edition. Crown 8vo, cloth, pp. x. and 567. 1890. Price 12s.
KEY to Ditto. Crown 8vo. cloth, pp. 126. Price 5s.

*RIOLA.—GRADUATED RUSSIAN READER, with a Vocabulary of all the Russian Words contained in it. By HENRY RIOLA. Crown 8vo, cloth, pp. viii. and 314. 1879. Price 10s. 6d.

THOMPSON.—DIALOGUES, RUSSIAN AND ENGLISH. Compiled by A. R. Thompson, some time Lecturer of the English Language in the University of St. Vladimir, Kieff. Crown 8vo, cloth, pp. iv. and 132. 1882. Price 5s.

SERBIAN.

MORFILL.—SIMPLIFIED GRAMMAR OF THE SERBIAN LANGUAGE. By W. R. MORFILL, M.A. Crown 8vo, cloth, pp. viii. and 72. 1887. Price 4s. 6d.

SPANISH.

*BUTLER.—THE SPANISH TEACHER AND COLLOQUIAL PHRASE-BOOK. An Easy and Agreeable Method of acquiring a Speaking Knowledge of the Spanish Language. By FRANCIS BUTLER. 18mo, half-roan, pp. xvi. and 240. 1870. Price 2s. 6d.

*CARRENO.—METODO PARA APRENDER A LEER, escribir y hablar el Inglés segun el sistema de Ollendorff, con un tratado de pronunciacion al principio y un Apendice importante al fin, que sirve de complemento a la obra. Por RAMON PALENZUELA Y JUAN DE LA CARREÑO. Nueva Edicion, con una Pronunciacion Figurada segun un Sistema Fonografico, por ROBERT GOODACRE. Crown 8vo, cloth, pp. iv. and 496. 1876. Price 4s. 6d.
KEY to Ditto. Crown 8vo, cloth, pp. 111. Price 3s.

HARTZENBUSCH and LEMMING.—ECO DE MADRID. A Practical Guide to Spanish Conversation. By J. E. HARTZENBUSCH and H. LEMMING. Third Edition. Crown 8vo, cloth, pp. xii., 144, and 84. 1877. Price 5s.

HARVEY.—SIMPLIFIED GRAMMAR OF THE SPANISH LANGUAGE. By W. F. HARVEY, M.A. Crown 8vo, cloth, pp. xii. and 49. 1890. Price 3s. 6d.

NOTLEY.—COMPARATIVE GRAMMAR OF THE FRENCH, ITALIAN, SPANISH, AND PORTUGUESE LANGUAGES. With a Copious Vocabulary. By EDWIN A. NOTLEY. Oblong 12mo, cloth, pp. xv. and 396. 1868. Price 7s. 6d.

*SIMONNE.—METODO PARA APRENDER A LEER, escribir y hablar el Frances, segun el verdadero sistema de Ollendorff; ordenado en lecciones progresivas, consistiendo de ejercicios orales y escritos ; enriquecido de la pronunciacion figurada como se estila en la conversacion ; y de un Apéndice abrazando las reglas de la sintáxis, la formacion de los

on Modern European Languages. 15

verbos regulares, y la conjugacion de los irregulares. Por TEODORO SIMONNE, Professor de Lenguas. Crown 8vo, cloth, pp. 342. 1876. Price 6s.
    KEY to Ditto. Crown 8vo, cloth, pp. 80. Price 3s. 6d.
*VELASQUEZ and SIMONNÉ.—NEW METHOD OF LEARNING TO READ, WRITE, AND SPEAK THE SPANISH LANGUAGE. Adapted to Ollendorff's System. By M. VELASQUEZ and J. SIMONNÉ. Revised and Corrected by Señor VIVAR. Crown 8vo, cloth, pp. 558. 1890. Price 6s.
    KEY to Ditto. Crown 8vo, cloth, pp. 174. Price 4s.
VELASQUEZ.—DICTIONARY OF THE SPANISH AND ENGLISH LANGUAGES. For the Use of Learners and Travellers. By M. VELASQUEZ DE LA CADENA. In Two Parts.—I. Spanish-English ; II. English-Spanish. Crown 8vo, cloth, pp. viii. and 846. 1890. Price 6s.
VELASQUEZ.—PRONOUNCING DICTIONARY OF THE SPANISH AND ENGLISH LANGUAGES. Composed from the Dictionaries of the Spanish Academy, Terreros, and Salvá, and Webster, Worcester, and Walker. In Two Parts.—I. Spanish-English ; II. English-Spanish. By M. VELASQUEZ DE LA CADENA. Royal 8vo, cloth, pp. xvi. and 675, xv. and 604. 1880. Price £1, 4s.
*VELASQUEZ.—NEW SPANISH READER. Passages from the most approved authors, in Prose and Verse. Arranged in progressive order, with Vocabulary. By M. VELASQUEZ DE LA CADENA. Crown 8vo, cloth, pp. 352. 1880. Price 6s.
*VELASQUEZ.—AN EASY INTRODUCTION TO SPANISH CONVERSATION, containing all that is necessary to make a rapid progress in it. Particularly designed for persons who have little time to study, or are their own instructors. By M. VELASQUEZ DE LA CADENA. Revised and Corrected by Señor VIVAR. 12mo, cloth, pp. viii. and 139. 1890. Price 2s. 6d.

SWEDISH.

NILSSON, WIDMARK, and COLLIN.—ENGLISH-SWEDISH DICTIONARY. Compiled by L. G. NILSSON, P. F. WIDMARK, and A. Z. COLLIN. New Edition. Demy 8vo, cloth, pp. iv. and 1304. 1889. Price 16s.
OMAN.—SVENSK-ENGELSK HAND-ORDBOK. (Swedish-English Dictionary.) By F. E. OMAN. Crown 8vo, cloth, pp. iv. and 470. 1872. Price 8s.
*OTTÉ.—SIMPLIFIED GRAMMAR OF THE SWEDISH LANGUAGE. By E. C. OTTÉ. Crown 8vo, pp. xii.-70, cloth. 1884. Price 2s. 6d.

TECHNICAL DICTIONARIES.

EGER.—TECHNOLOGICAL DICTIONARY IN THE ENGLISH AND GERMAN LANGUAGES. Edited by GUSTAV EGER, Professor of the Polytechnic School of Darmstadt, and Sworn Translator of the Grand Ducal Ministerial Departments. Technically revised and enlarged by OTTO BRANDES, Chemist. 2 vols., royal 8vo, cloth, pp. viii. and 712, and pp. viii. and 970. 1884. £1, 7s.
KARMARSCH.—TECHNOLOGICAL DICTIONARY OF THE TERMS EMPLOYED IN THE ARTS AND SCIENCES; Architecture, Civil, Military, and Naval ; Civil Engineering ; Mechanics ; Machine Making ; Shipbuilding and Navigation ; Metallurgy ; Artillery ; Mathematics ;

Physics; Chemistry; Mineralogy, &c. With a Preface by Dr. K. KARMARSCH. Third Edition. 3 vols.
Vol. I. German-English-French. 8vo, cloth, pp. 646. Price 12s.
Vol. II. English-German-French. 8vo, cloth, pp. 666. Price 12s.
Vol. III. French-German-English. 8vo, cloth, pp. 618. Price 15s.

VEITELLE.—MERCANTILE DICTIONARY. A Complete Vocabulary of the Technicalities of Commercial Correspondence, Names of Articles of Trade, and Marine Terms, in English, Spanish, and French; with Geographical Names, Business Letters, and Tables of the Abbreviations in Common Use in the three Languages. By I. DE VEITELLE. Crown 8vo, cloth, pp. 303. Price 7s. 6d.

TURKISH.

ARNOLD.—SIMPLE TRANSLITERAL GRAMMAR OF THE TURKISH LANGUAGE. Compiled from Various Sources. With Dialogues and Vocabulary. By Sir EDWIN ARNOLD, M.A., K.C.I.E., C.S.I., F.R.G.S. 18mo, cloth, pp. 80. 1877. Price 2s. 6d.

HOPKINS.—ELEMENTARY GRAMMAR OF THE TURKISH LANGUAGE. With a Few Easy Exercises. By F. L. HOPKINS, M.A., Fellow and Tutor of Trinity Hall, Cambridge. Crown 8vo, cloth, pp. 48. 1877. Price 3s. 6d.

REDHOUSE.—THE TURKISH VADE-MECUM OF OTTOMAN COLLOQUIAL LANGUAGE: Containing a Concise Ottoman Grammar; a Carefully Selected Vocabulary, Alphabetically Arranged, in Two Parts, English and Turkish, and Turkish and English; also a Few Familiar Dialogues and Naval and Military Terms. The whole in English Characters, the Pronunciation being fully indicated. By J. W. REDHOUSE, M.R.A.S. Third Edition. Fourth Thousand. 32mo, cloth, pp. viii. and 368. 1882. Price 6s.

*REDHOUSE.—A SIMPLIFIED GRAMMAR OF THE OTTOMAN TURKISH LANGUAGE. By J. W. REDHOUSE, M.R.A.S. Crown 8vo, cloth, pp. xii. and 204. 1884. Price 10s. 6d.

REDHOUSE.—A TURKISH AND ENGLISH LEXICON. Showing in English the Signification of the Turkish Terms. By J. W. REDHOUSE, M.R.A.S. Parts I. to III. Imperial 8vo, paper covers, pp. 960. 1884-85. Price 27s.

WELSH.

EVANS.—A DICTIONARY OF THE WELSH LANGUAGE. By the Rev. D. SILVAN EVANS, B.D., Rector of Llanwrin, Machynlleth, North Wales. Part I., A—AWYS. Royal 8vo, paper, pp. 420. Price 10s. 6d. Part II., B—BYW. Royal 8vo, paper, pp. 192. Price 5s.

LONDON: KEGAN PAUL, TRENCH, TRÜBNER, & CO., LT?
1 PATERNOSTER SQUARE, AND 57 & 59 LUDGATE HILL.

PRINTED BY BALLANTYNE, HANSON AND CO.
EDINBURGH AND LONDON.

www.ingramcontent.com/pod-product-compliance
Lightning Source LLC
Chambersburg PA
CBHW021940160426
43195CB00011B/1164